CATTLEMAN

RAYMOND KEOGH

CATTLEMAN

RAYMOND KEOGH

as told to
GUY WILLIAMS

SOMERVILLE PRESS

Somerville Press,
Dromore, Bantry,
Co. Cork, Ireland

ISBN: 978 0 9562231 7 3

Printed and bound by GraphyCems,
Villatuerta, Navarra, Spain

Contents

Foreword

I welcome this excellent story of creative cattlemen Jack Keogh and Raymond Keogh, father and son. Their lives interacted with the evolution of the Irish economy through the twentieth and into the twenty-first century.

Jack Keogh came from a family of traditional livestock traders. They had a firm commercial foundation that grew out of business competence.

Jack detected the relative decline of live exports and their replacement by the carcase trade. He initially associated with Gerard Counihan who built on the grand scale but lacked the matching mettle. Later followed a profitable link with Frank Quinn and others in creating a massive meat business at Leixlip. The dominant partner was Frank Quinn who initiated the sale to Cork Marts. The Cork failure was founded on inexperience and perhaps over-confidence. In his story, Raymond Keogh has dealt kindly with that venture. We are also given the forgotten story of Ireland's first commercial meat plant at Roscrea. It was established by the Crowley family and by a German, George Fasenfeld. Roscrea provided a profitable outlet for Ireland's cull cows. Over 200,000 yearly in numbers, they had no developed market. Many just died of old age on the farm.

Raymond's career was more centred on the carcase trade and on livestock financing. The family were central in founding Livestock Credit with James Bastow. It was highly successful in providing capital for farmers who were under-stocked due to lack of credit. There may have been questions on the interest rate charged yet there was a margin for farmer and financier – far better than understocked land. Serious risks were not incurred and the company had thousands of satisfied customers.

The story of Charolais and other European breed imports is told in graphic and accurate detail. It is hard to believe that official policy maintained protracted opposition to valuable cattle. An active campaign was necessary to move the civil servants.

In his capacity as a Co. Meath farmer, Raymond Keogh became Master of the Ward Union Hunt. Management of the pack was superb. Followers had good sport, always with some element of personal danger. The quarry, deer, were very seldom killed and the so called elements of cruelty were not part of the hunt's ethos.

Personally, I found the careful hunting over land was exemplary. Growing crops were avoided. Headlands were used where developed and where available. A bypass was used as the ultimate alternative. A small minority did not accept the hunt and their wishes were respected. Children of non-hunting farmers were encouraged, trained and facilitated to participate. Raymond Keogh sought to have the Ward Union farmer friendly – a feeling that was reciprocated.

In his own words, this lifetime review 'covers the entire sweep of Irish farming' as experienced in the past 100 years. The story is very well told.

Paddy O'Keeffe
February 2012

CHAPTER ONE

Background

'Keogh is a quintessentially Gaelic surname.' Thus does Ida Grehan open her essay on my family in her *Irish Family Histories*. We were to be found principally in Tipperary, in Roscommon and latterly in Wicklow as bards to the O'Byrnes. John Keogh (1746–1817) was a pioneer of Catholic emancipation, though he did not live to see it. Myles Keogh (1848–1876), a career soldier, survived several wars, only to throw in his lot with Colonel George Custer. He perished with his leader and 600 others at the massacre of Little Big Horn, where the Sioux got one back under their leader Crazy Horse. Ironically, the only survivor was Keogh's horse, Comanche. He was duly rescued and revered for twenty years. On his death, Comanche was stuffed and put on display in the Kansas University Museum.

Before Myles Keogh became involved in what might be termed the 'buffalo wars' that cost him his young life, James Keogh had set his store by bullocks. *Griffith's Valuation* (1854) lists James Keogh, my great-grandfather, as tenant of over 150 acres of land in the townlands of Ballyhack and Primatestown in the parish of Kilmoon in north County Dublin. William Loftus Keogh, a kinsman, is listed as owner and tenant of another 100 acres of land in Painestown, in the adjoining parish of Macestown. John Keogh, likewise related, held almost as much land in the same vicinity.

James Keogh was a grazier; one who bought 'store' cattle—principally bullocks for the export trade—at fairs throughout the country, consigning them by rail to either Fairyhouse halt or Clonee station, whence they were driven to his farms for 'finishing' on the summer meadows. When summer turned to autumn and grass grew scarce the livestock, by then 'finished' and ready for slaughter were driven on foot to the Dublin City market—then staged in Smithfield—to be sold.

What might appear a straightforward, foolproof *modus operandi* is belied by a summary of his son John Keogh's assets and liabilities: 'On May the 4th 1888 John Keogh had 212 cattle on the grass worth £12 each, and nothing for them to eat.'

In due course James was joined by his son Christopher Jacob (born c.1850), who expanded the family involvement in the cattle trade by taking a stall in the market. In addition, Christopher leased properties at Cabra, Ashtown and Inchicore, all with holding paddocks (lairage) within easy reach of the Dublin Corporation's cattle market, which had been transferred from its historic location in Smithfield to the North Circular Road. He was thus in a position to sell not just the Keogh cattle, but livestock belonging to others. His position in the marketplace further enabled him to begin buying, on commission, for the English wholesale butchers who would cross the Irish Sea on the cattle boats from Birkenhead, fill their orders and return that same day with their purchases.

Christopher's diversification in 1902 coincided with the birth of his eldest son, John—invariably called Jack—who left the Garristown national school aged 12 to become the third generation Keogh to carry on the cattle business. Christopher and his wife—a Collins from County Clare—went on to have three further sons. Julius went into partnership with Jack, only to fall out with his elder brother and die a bachelor after a lifetime dogged by depression. Jarlath joined the British Army, dying young from the delayed effects of being gassed on the Western Front. His descendants settled in Wales. Christopher junior lived in Finnstown House, Lucan, an hotel in more recent times. Of their two sisters, May Keogh enlisted in the British Army and died unmarried. Clare Keogh married Richard James Hayes, of whom more anon.

Christopher based himself in Cabra Villa, Finglas, a sizeable house, the leasehold having been held for the previous 400 years by the Rathborne family, candlemakers and the oldest company in Ireland. His household was extended to include his nephews James and John Byrne. James, a handsome and talented young man, became his uncle's bookkeeper. James was to later to provide a pen portrait of his great-uncle James Keogh of Ballyhack, grazier. Stocky, of medium height, James Keogh was clean-shaven, wore breeches and woollen stockings. While he never smoked—unusually for his era—he was partial to a glass of whiskey. Returning home from Smithfield, James was in the habit of slaking his thirst in hostelries along the way. He invariably stood a drink for every man present, justifying this practice by declaring it 'a cheap way of earning the reputation as a generous man.' By James Byrne's account James Keogh died from excessive blood pressure, adamant that he would do so intestate. Anne, his widow, outlived him by twenty years.

John Byrne, a well-built six-footer and *bon viveur*, quickly gained a reputation as a skilled nagsman. Uncle Christy—an acknowledged judge of horseflesh—spotted and bought working horses at fairs around the country. John then schooled them under saddle before demonstrating their ability with the Ward Union Staghounds, then, as now, an ideal showcase from which to sell on the Dublin customers happy to pay for a 'made' conveyance to carry them safely over the yawning ditches that characterize the Ward country.

A showman to his fingertips, sporting a white topper, Christopher Keogh drove a matched pair of greys in a gig—not side-by side but in tandem—from Cabra Villa to visit his mother in Curragha, making the round trip in two hours or less. His journey also took in Hollywood Rath, where he had rented the grazing. On one such trip he proffered a cheery salute to a bystander as his equipage bore him through Ratoath at a spanking trot, oblivious to the bystander's identity.

Not recognizing the driver, the bystander mentioned to the Ward Union huntsman that he had just received a grand salute from 'Thunder Lagore'. The Thunder family were large landowners in Lagore, close to Ratoath, hence the nickname. Bemused, the huntsman rejoined that the only passer-by he had seen was Christy Keogh, whom the saluted one vehemently detested. Cross beyond measure, the latter expostulated: 'I wouldn't have wished that for a thousand pounds!'

In a country where 'nothing fails like success', Christopher Keogh had achieved social status whereby he was on speaking terms with such notables among the landowning gentry as Lord Ashtown and his son the Hon. Willie Trench, Edward 'Cub' Kennedy of Bishopscourt, William Wallace of Ballymacarney and the Leonards, tenants-in-chief of some 7,000 acres from Lord Fingal. The Leonards would only buy hunters on Christy Keogh's recommendation.

Besides gaining entrée to the predominantly Church of Ireland sporting set, Christy and his family elevated their standing among their own through having a priest in the family. That was Thomas, Christy's brother, who had received his training in Rome prior to becoming curate to the celebrated wit Fr Healy of Little Bray. Further family respectability was acquired when their sister took holy orders as Sister Gracias. She spent most of her ordained life working in mental institutions in France, speaking fluent French, without ever losing her broad Meath accent.

When I escaped from the tender mercies of the Society of Jesus, Clongowes Wood, in 1947 all I ever wanted to do was to follow in the footsteps of my father Jack, grandfather Christy and great-grandfather James into the cattle business, the fourth generation Keogh so to do. To be fair to my mentors in Clongowes, I had no interest in the passport to the recognized professions that they offered. Their aspirations for their pupils and my personal ambitions simply travelled on parallel tracks. And while parallels are said to meet in infinity, for a sixteen-year-old, starry-eyed youth, 'infinity' was quite time enough.

CHAPTER TWO
Cattle Trade History

Anyone spending a lifetime in any particular business or profession tends to assume a similar degree of knowledge on the part of his reader. In my case, the anxiety to flee the halls of academe and return to the hustle, bustle, banter and business of the cattle trade effectively prevented me ever exploring its origins in Ireland. Indeed, it was not until I had effectively retired after a lifetime's involvement that I became curious to explore what lay in the past, underpinning the all-consuming present.

Fortunately for me, increased leisure time and mounting curiosity coincided more or less with the publication in 2003 of John Feehan's intriguing tome—*Farming in Ireland – History, Heritage and Environment*. Never an avid reader, I initially baulked at its sheer size, over 500 pages. All right, I have to confess that my bargain-driving background rebelled at the outlay involved. Imagine, paying the thick end of a 'ton' for a book, and only a tenner back to make it lucky!

The illustrations made me waver, but it was the blurb that won me over. 'This is the first book to look at the entire sweep of Irish farming through its long history, focusing in particular on the way farming has shaped the natural and cultural endowment of the island, and reviewing the state of that endowment today. Successive chapters review the main phases of Ireland's farming history from the arrival of the first farmers some 6,500 years ago.'

'Put it there,' said I to the bewildered cashier, forgetting that I was no longer shaking hands on a deal with a 'horny-handed son of the soil', but instead handing over a ransom that held out no prospect of a return. Well, who ever heard tell of a book that gained value, be it grass-fattened or stall-fed? Actually, it was one of the best deals I ever did strike. Had I been given *Farming in Ireland* as a present it would have adorned a coffee table until displaced by another of similar size and appearance. However, having cost half a year's agricultural worker's wage as it was when I started out, this book was going to teach me more than the Jesuits ever did.

In the same way that a racing man's newspaper unfailingly opens at the racing page, so did *Farming in Ireland* tend to do at the sections relating to cattle. Well, a clearcut table of contents helped in that regard. It disclosed that cattle had first appeared in Ireland almost 4,000 years before St Patrick. They might have got here earlier had they not proved the most difficult of the four main meat sources to be 'domesticated'. Goats became the first, followed by sheep and then pigs. Cows, it seems, proved contrary, as anyone who has ever tried to drive cows in any direction other than the one they are accustomed to travel will tell you with feeling. Should you ever have the time and inclination to do so, observe a dairy herd returning to the milking parlour. The herd forms a line in its accustomed pecking order, which is scrupulously maintained right up to the point of entry and never varies. Each cow has its appointed place and woe betide anyone foolish enough to intervene.

The first cows in Ireland are thought to have been black and small by present standards. Irish place names such as Inisbofin and Lake Bofin suggest that black cows were followed by white cows. Whether these two went on to breed brown cows in addition to black-and-white cows is a moot point. What is known is that they were very slow to mature by modern standards, only producing their first calf when aged four. Sir William Wilde—Oscar's father—when writing in 1835 'On the ancient and modern races of oxen in Ireland' divided the Irish cow population into four categories. He wrote of the 'old Irish cow', the Kerry cow, the longhorn and the 'Maol' or 'moyle', meaning hornless.

This is how Wilde described the Irish longhorn—found mainly in the western midlands. 'The Irish longhorns—resembling the Lancashire and the Craven; in some cases the horns were wide-spreading and only slightly curved, but frequently the horns were so completely curved inwards as to cross in front of or behind the mouth, or pressed inward so much towards the cheek as to become a great source of irritation to the animal, and to require amputation; they were generally a red or brindled colour, had large bones, grew to a great size, particularly as bullocks, and their drooping horns, sloping gracefully under the skin, gave them a particularly calm expression of face: they were covered with a plentiful supply of hair . . . an exceedingly hardy race of cattle, never requiring fodder except when the ground was covered with snow . . . not much used as milkers; they were the principal cattle sent to the Dublin market or exported thirty years ago; their hides were of great value . . . they might justly be termed "the Connaught ox".'

Curiously, less that 50 years later 'the Connaught ox' was on the verge of extinction. In 1872 one writer instanced this remarkable rapid decline of the Irish longhorn. 'The last time I saw longhorns exhibited in public was at the Spring Show of the Royal Dublin Society, in 1858, when Lord de Freyne exhibited a pair of two-year-old oxen in the fat stock classes; and so little was the breed known then that I recall some persons present enquiring what "foreign breed" Lord de Freyne's bullocks belonged to.'

As the Irish longhorn was destined to vanish into the mists of time, so too the 'old Irish cow'. I feel it only right that she get her space here, as William Wilde described this animal on which so many Irish families depended for their very survival. 'The Old Irish Cow—

of small stature, long in the back, with moderate sized, wide-spreading slightly elevated and projecting horns; they could scarcely be called long-horned, and they are certainly not short-horned; this breed was of all colours, but principally black and red. They were famous milkers, easily fed, extraordinarily gentle, requiring little care, and were, in truth, the poor man's cow . . . but they did not fatten easily, and when beyond a certain age seldom put on flesh; they abounded in all parts of the plain country.'

In the decades that followed further breeds—Devons, Dexters, Durham crosses, Herefords and Shorthorns were introduced to Ireland, some for milk and others for meat, overcoming an ancient reluctance to butcher cattle except as a last resort. As time went by the new breeds came to dominate the national herd to the point at which the Kerry cow became the only one of Wilde's four categories to survive as a separate and distinct entity. That the Kerry was alone in this regard was due to its ability to survive and provide milk on the poorest and harshest terrain, like its recently-classified grazing companion, the Kerry bog pony.

Long before that cows were the measure of wealth in Ireland, as confirmed by the 'Táin Bó Cúailnge', otherwise the 'Cattle Raid of Cooley'. In fact cows remained the currency of this country until the end of the sixteenth century. Proof is to be found in the compensation paid to the Earl of Kildare in 1554 for the slaying of his brother-in-law. The 'blood price' was 340 cows. English documents from the 1570s refer to two known herds of over 50,000 cattle in Irish hands, one belonging to the Earl of Dungannon, the other to Sorley Boy MacDonnell. Twenty years later the Earl of Tyrone's power and influence was assessed on his herd of cows, estimated to number 120,000 milking cows.

By the end of the sixteenth century currency had begun to take the place of livestock, with a cow being worth £1. However, long before that change from cows to currency, Ireland had begun to ship live cattle to England, the origins of this country's export economy. The English dubbed these unruly creatures 'Wicke Kayne', glad though they were to butcher and eat same 'wild kine'.

The Irish beef trade continued to thrive and prosper—Oliver Cromwell's Irish tour notwithstanding—until 1666, when the Restoration Parliament bowed to pressure from English beef producers to impose a ban on all beef imports from Ireland; the Cattle Acts. Denied their only market, Irish beef producers faced ruin, a prospect that brought native ingenuity quickly into play. Instead they began to salt beef, veal, butter and bacon in barrels, exporting these preserved products to Spain, to France and to the burgeoning American Colonies. Happily, the repeal of those punitive Cattle Acts in 1760 led to an immediate resumption of live exports to England, with an attendant expansion of production of stores and fat cattle.

That development had a profound effect on the Irish countryside. Specialized breeding and finishing areas developed, cattle moved in a clockwise sweep from their birthplace in the dairying lands of Munster through the western counties' rearing lands to the fattening pastures of Meath, Kildare and Dublin. Cattle were bought to be sold and sold to buy replacements, their husbandry trade becoming the primary skills of the vast majority of Irish farmers. The importance of cattle commerce was reflected in the explosion of cattle fairs from 700 in the seventeenth century through 3,000 in the eighteenth and an astonishing 5,000 just before the Great Famine of 1847.

Kevin Whelan painted this evocative word picture in his contribution to the *Atlas of the Irish Rural Landscape*. 'In cattle-fattening areas grazier holdings became the cornerstone of leasing policy and of settlement patterns. Given its extensive mode of land use, the grazier economy created a barren landscape with an attenuated social structure and only rudimentary settlement forms, where the lonely box-Georgian graziers' houses were juxtaposed with the crude cabins of the herds. The large silent fields of grazing bullocks were anomalous in an Irish world which elsewhere was so noisy, crowded and complex. In counties Meath and Kildare it was common in the late eighteenth century for 400 or 600 hectares to be in the hands of a single grazier. In the grazing baronies of Carra, Kilmaine and Clanmaurice in Mayo the average field size on grazier holdings in 1800 was forty hectares.'

It appears that our forebears treasured the cow for her dairy products—milk, butter and cheese—whereas beef was seen as an export commodity, be it dead or alive. However, healthy cattle, both male and female, could be and were used as a source of food, as one horrified John O'Donovan recounted while engaged in fieldwork for the Ordnance Survey in 1834, writing from Draperstown, County Derry.

'The inhabitants of Muintirloney in Tyrone and Ballynascreen retain an old custom that has quite astonished me. They are in the habit of bleeding their cattle and using the blood as food. I have made every enquiry to see how far this practice prevails, and I have learned from sources of undoubted veracity that the farmers and graziers continue bleeding their bullocks, cows and heifers from the beginning of May until the 20th of August, a period during which the cattle are well fed and able to bear bleeding. A strong bullock would bear to give three quarts [approx 3 litres] of the red stream of life at a time. This is settled in the tub until it congeals and is preserved for use for four or five days by salting it. It is prepared for use by taking home lumps of the clotted fluid and placing them in a pot when the water is near the boiling point, but if the water should be boiling at the time of the immersion it will not do. When the blood is sufficiently boiled it is taken up and mixed with butter, and variously prepared according to the taste or knowledge of the cook, and is considered a great luxury by the mountaineers. The cattle are improved, not injured by being thus bled, and the blood serves the mountaineers for flesh-meat. This was a great source of food to the inhabitants in ancient times. I have exclaimed against this practice before the provost Mac Namee, who states that he often bled cattle and ate the blood himself.

'I think that this is the most abominable custom that ever prevailed among any people, but perhaps I am inclined to think so from association of ideas, and from prejudices of my own fancy. Does Mr McCloskey mention this practice in his MSS? I could not bear the idea of using the blood of any animal yet living, but the inhabitants of this district deem it similar to using the milk of cows. What think you of this custom?

'I am glad to learn from your note that you agree with me upon the barbarity of the custom of boiling and eating the blood of living animals. The manner in which Mr McCloskey mentions it would lead a person to believe that the herds in the hard summer of 1817 were driven by necessity to draw and boil the blood of the cattle placed under their care; but the fact is otherwise. The custom is continued in Muintirloney to this day.

'The bullocks and heifers are bled for the improvement of their health, and the blood is cooked and used as food, not through necessity, but as a luxury; and they contend that it is as lawful and as civilized to use their blood as their milk, and that the blood taken from a healthy heifer or bullock while living is as clean and fit to be used as the blood of any animal when dead. I have spoken to the Revd Manus O'Kane upon this subject. He condemns the custom as barbarous to his ideas, but sees no sound reason or authority for condemning it.

'Mr McCloskey was either ashamed of the custom, or he was misinformed upon the extent and obstinacy of it, for the people are not only not ashamed of it but unwilling to discontinue it, because they insist that it is perfectly civilized and proper.'

I thought I should include that nugget from *Cattle in Ancient Ireland*, not just to demonstrate my recently-acquired erudition in such matters, but really to show that the herdsmen of the Kenyan plains have more in common with our own than many of us perhaps appreciate.

What did survive that sudden switch from salted exports to cattle on the hook once more was the butter business, becoming Ireland's biggest agricultural export by the end of the eighteenth century. Established in 1770, the Cork Butter Exchange grew into what was said to be the largest centre of its kind in the world. Its *modus operandi* was described thus in 1852. 'Every firkin of butter that passes through the old Cork Weigh-Houses—and nearly every firkin that enters this city passes through it—is rigidly examined and its quality determined, and when this butter is received by the foreign buyer he has a sufficient guarantee as to the character and quality of the article in the well-known brand upon its cask. Butter is graded between first and sixth quality. In this way the farmer, the merchant, and the foreign buyer are equally protected against fraud.'

Traditionally butter had been made on the farm by the woman of the house to use for barter or for sale, in the same way that she would subsequently utilize poultry and eggs. It was the development of the creameries under Sir Horace Plunkett's co-operative movement (the Irish Agricultural Organization Society) that created a more structured and more rewarding butter industry. By 1900 there were 236 Dairy Societies with 26,577 members, whose profits were said to have increased thereby from 30% to 35%.

The attempts to create a 'rural civilization' were intended to benefit the entire rural community, as outlined by one of the movement's pioneers, R.A. Anderson. 'A very pleasing feature in the development of the creamery system is the opportunity it has given to labourers to become cow owners. Numbers of them now have cows, and one case has been reported where a man living in an ordinary way-side cottage with one acre of land has been enabled to own eight milch cows, from the milk of which he has realized £70 in cash during the last year. From grazing one cow by the roadside—on the 'long farm' as it is called in the country—he was enabled to buy additional cows and rent grazing for them through the profits he derived from the Creamery.'

While that picture paints an image of rustic bliss and self-betterment, it was, in time, to provide the genesis of the Livestock Credit Corporation, financing the hire-purchase of cows. But we will come to that in due course.

As this is only intended as a thumbnail sketch of the history of cattle in Ireland it will suffice to say that in 2003, when *Farming in Ireland* was published by UCD's Faculty of Agriculture, the national herd stood at 7,000,000, with a further 1,700,000 head in the Six Counties. In a country that prides itself as a world leader in thoroughbred horse production and training, it is all too easy to overlook the crucial contribution to Ireland's balance of payments provided by the cloven-hoofed species.

CHAPTER THREE
1902–1932

The Dublin cattle market, where my grandfather Christy Keogh leased a stall in 1902, had moved not many years before from its centuries-old location in Stoneybatter. Curiously, the opening of that earlier cattle market coincided with the Cattle Acts, which had dramatically closed the English market to importation of cattle from Ireland. Douglas Bennett provided a colourful pen portrait of what later became an inner-city market in his *Encyclopaedia of Dublin*. 'In the 1660s, a large cattle market was opened and, throughout the eighteenth and nineteenth centuries, there was a concentration of dairies in the area, with cows being milked in back yards, and carts with large churns selling milk around the city. In the 1760s, fashionable houses were built in the area near Oxmantown Green as it still had a rural feel to it. During the eighteenth century, a festival was held on May Day when large crowds danced around a pole covered in garlands. This ceased in 1773 when unruly soldiers from the Royal Barracks, built in 1701–06, attempted to pull down the pole. Amid scuffles, shots were fired and the residents decided that it was no longer safe to hold a festival each year.'

John Warburton brought the depiction of Smithfield up to 1818, when his *History of Dublin* was published. Smithfield was then the great wholesale market for hay and cattle and by Warburton's reckoning 30,000 head of cattle were bought and sold here annually, a considerable number of them for export. However, the approaches to Smithfield were so narrow and difficult that the passages were often choked up with beasts, while the haycarts had to be left on the outskirts, their contents frequently pilfered. Besides Smithfield there were nine other established markets in the various parishes, generally in poor areas with insufficient ventilation. As cattle were usually killed on the spot, there being no public abattoirs, they were houses of horror flowing with offal and ordure. Warburton quoted from an 1806 report on prevailing conditions. 'Several very offensive nuisances exist in the City of Dublin such as dairies, slaughter-houses and the practice of throwing dirt and offal, etc., out of the markets at night. It appears in evidence that none of the said dairies or slaughter-houses are provided with sewers, or any other means of preserving cleanliness, in consequence of which the filth is accumulated in the most noxious and offensive manner, and frequently spreads over the adjoining streets, occasioning the most intolerable stench imaginable.'

If that were not bad enough, it appears that the cattle markets, as well as the streets, were also theatres for bull-baiting, which sometimes led to riots. Moreover, cruelty was practised by drovers that defied belief, as one English observer reported. 'I was frequently shocked at the cruelties exercised by the "penny boys" as they are called, who drive cattle from Smithfield to slaughter. They are permitted by police, contrary to the Act of the legislature, to carry bludgeons, with which they beat and batter the legs of sheep in particular in a manner the most savage that can be conceived.'

Stoneybatter covers the area from Smithfield, Prussia Street and the North Circular Road...Substitute 'Smithfield' for 'Stoneybatter' and make the mental leap from 1773 to first decade of the twenty-first century and perhaps acknowledge the depth of wisdom in a phrase coined by our French friends—'*plus ça change, plus c'est la même*'.

I digress. Christy Keogh took an office and a cattle pen on the North Circular Road, where the cattle market was clearly in existence pre-1882. Justification for saying as much is once again provided by Douglas Bennett, who revealed that Dublin Corporation, concerned by the number of unhygienic slaughter houses in operation within the city precincts, commissioned a new abattoir (in 1882), designed by Park Neville, on ten acres outside the North Circular Road, divided by the cattle market. However, as it was outside the city boundary, the Corporation could not compel Dublin butchers to use it, resulting in its closure within a few years.

Irrespective of where they had their cattle killed, those same Dublin butchers still had to procure the cattle in question, which they did from the cattle market beside the North Circular Road. Christy Keogh was but one of many intent on satisfying this continuous demand. He was soon joined by his son Jack, my father, who was only too glad to exchange the drudgery of the classroom for the adrenaline of the cattle business, where speech and drama, together with a keen grasp of elementary maths, were the key to survival, hopefully success.

The First World War, with its voracious appetite for men, munitions, horses and foodstuffs constituted a bonanza for Irish farmers. The British Government's failure to introduce price controls—as it was to do in the Second World War—made the cattle trade in particular a seller's market. Agricultural land soared to an unthinkable £100 an acre. The Counihan family was just an example of many entrepreneurs who seized this opportunity to prosper. Four flamboyant brothers, whose enterprise more than concealed their initial lack of ready money, leased no less than 1,000 acres of the Lyons estate from Lord Cloncurry. On the strength of that credit-inducing stratagem they persuaded an impressionable bank manager to advance them the money to pay a deposit to his lordship, and to stock the lands. By the time that war drew to its exhausted close the Counihan brothers had made enough to buy a farm each—Turvey, Beechlawn, Skidoo and one the name of which escapes me.

As the Keoghs remained uninvolved in politics so did they weather the turmoil of the 1916 Easter Rising and the War of Independence that followed. In so far as those events affected their busy lives they did so to the extent of disruptions to the vital rail network, which frequently frustrated the transport of livestock from the fairs throughout Ireland to the North Circular Road.

Inevitably, as had happened when previous military campaigns concluded, the boom years of the First World War were followed by recession. As the demand for cattle collapsed, so did the value of agricultural land. Strong farmers, once the backbone of banks all over Ireland, had suddenly to cut their coats to suit their cloth, grandiose expansion plans brought to a shuddering halt. That the fledgling Free State Government had to turn to Jacobs and Guinness to guarantee its promissory notes was a measure of Ireland's economic stagnation.

It was into this trough of despondency that I came into the world on 5 January 1931. And, in accordance with the old adage that a birth so often precipitates a death within the family, Christy Keogh, my grandfather, passed away the following year, aged 82. Unlike his father before him, Christy did leave his affairs in order. Jack, my father, was left the cattle market concern he had shared with his father for almost two decades, while Christy, my uncle, was bequeathed three parcels of land—Money Hill, New Haggard and The Bog—amounting to 70 acres all told.

In the same year that my grandfather went to meet his Maker, the Irish Government—Cumann na nGaedheal—was voted out of office for the first time since the inception of the Irish Free State in 1922. Irish political history is hardly my forte, though what I understand is that growing impatience with Ireland's stagnant economy persuaded the Irish people to dump the founding government and throw in its lot with one Eamon de Valera, leader of the Fianna Fáil party, notwithstanding its links with the IRA.

The *New York Times* correspondent assigned to cover that historic 1932 general election contrasted William Cosgrave 'cold and unromantic, with no attraction for Irish youth,' with the de Valera campaign, 'arousing emotions strangely like those Adolf Hitler is spreading through Germany . . . Anything but a firebrand, this mild, academic, lean and tight-lipped, who lectures his audience and leaves it to his lieutenants to revive emotions of more troubled times.'

James Dillon, newly-elected Independent Nationalist TD for Donegal, left an imperishable description of his first day in the Dáil. 'The feeling in Dáil Éireann when I first arrived in it in 1932 was quite extraordinary. A very considerable number of the Fianna Fáil party arrived in the Dáil on the day Mr de Valera was first elected, armed to the teeth. They thought there was going to be a putsch, that if Mr de Valera was elected Mr Cosgrave wouldn't hand over Government. They had a completely illusory notion of the standards and character of Mr Cosgrave, who, of course, had brought—indeed forced—Fianna Fáil into Dáil Éireann in order to establish normal political functioning in the country. So they were swaggering around the place with revolvers bulging out of their pockets. One old gentleman was assembling a machine-gun in a telephone booth.'

Fianna Fáil—the 'slightly constitutional party'—had come to power on its election manifesto of economic and constitutional revolution. It proposed to abolish the Oath of Allegiance (to the English monarchy) and suspend the payment of land annuities immediately, provoking certain conflict with Britain. Furthermore, Fianna Fáil promised to embark on an ambitious policy to promote tillage at the direct expense of the livestock business. 'The bullock for the road; the land for the people.'

CHAPTER FOUR

Formative Years

When I came into this world, in January 1931, followed at intervals by my sisters Gertrude, Christina and Marie, our family lived in 114 Lindsay Road, Glasnevin, home to my father Jack Keogh and his wife Anna (née Sheridan, Ballybar House, Carlow). Built from about 1904, Lindsay Road runs parallel to the better known, posher Iona Road. Though the houses (red brick) on both streets were built by Alexander Strain and thus of the best quality, the fact that one side of Lindsay Road backed on to the railway line tended to lower the status of the street as a whole. Interestingly, this is borne out in the 1911 census, which described Iona Road as being a mixture of first and second class houses. The 74 houses on Lindsay Road at that stage were all classified in the lower category, many of them with fowl houses attached. Nonetheless, they were described as 'both looking well, extremely well-equipped and comfortable, with the added luxuries of a bathroom . . . and indoor lavatory'. They originally sold for between £425 and £500, depending on whether the attic had been converted, by the inclusion of a further staircase, to make another room.

Of my early years in Glasnevin I have little recall. Indeed, it was not until I joined my father in his business that I achieved any understanding of the calamitous effects of that 1932 General Election which saw Eamon de Valera and his Fianna Fáil party take over the reins of government. Fianna Fáil's election promises were based on a strategy of economic protectionism which blithely ignored the stark fact that the export of live cattle to Britain was the backbone of Ireland's economy. Jack Keogh's livelihood was correspondingly blighted.

Since the foundation of the Irish Free State in 1922 the peaceful continuation of that vital commerce depended on the payment of land annuities to the British government; agreed compensation for the redistribution of Irish land from its English landlords to Irish tenant farmers. It amounted to £3 million annually. The moment Fianna Fáil implemented that election promise the British retaliated by imposing tariffs on all agricultural imports from the Irish Free State. De Valera's answer was to impose corresponding tariffs on British coal, cement and other manufactured products.

This battle became known as the Economic War, a struggle from which there could only ever be one winner. Whereas Britain was relatively unaffected, the Irish economy was crippled. The tariff on live cattle was initially £2 per head, which rose to £4 and then to £6. As England was then going through its own economic depression the price of cattle was very low, down from the wartime high to as little as £16 a head. By the time the English buyer factored in his £6 tariff, that left the Irish vendor looking at £10 per head, or £1 per hundredweight.

Cattle exports to Britain plummeted from 750,000 in 1930 to 500,000 in 1934. Well, so the official figures would say. However, human ingenuity in the face of adversity soon gave rise to a thriving cross-border smuggling business. It was reckoned to account for 100,000 head finding their way to Britain in 1935 alone. Some surprisingly prominent Unionist figures were linked to this practice. Meanwhile, Irish unemployment soared from 29,000 in 1931 to 96,000 in 1933 and again to hit 138,000 by 1935. Incredibly, two general elections were fought and won by Fianna Fáil, whose supporters voted in sufficient numbers to maintain this state of economic suicide. Fortunately, de Valera began to come to his senses as emigration swelled to levels unseen since the famine years of the 1840s. For those who had no choice but to remain, agricultural wages had fallen to 8 shillings a week, barely sufficient for survival.

In 1934 the Coal-Cattle pact relaxed matters and in 1938 the Anglo-Irish Trade Agreement resolved that vexed issue of the land annuities, when the Irish government consented to a once-off payment of £10 million. If you've ever wondered at that extraordinary statistic whereby more Irish—be they first, second or third generation—are to be found in the Greater Liverpool area than in the whole of the 26 Counties, now you know.

None of this meant anything to me as a boarder in the Presentation Convent in Cabra. You might think it strange that an order of nuns taught little boys as boarders in what was a mixed school. But they did, as indeed did their counterparts in Kilashee, near Naas, up to the 1970s. When I had turned ten, during the Second World War, my parents decided to send me to the Jesuits in Clongowes Wood. I learned afterwards that their decision was influenced by the remarkable results obtained in that academy by my uncle-by-marriage, Doctor Richard James Hayes, who had been appointed Director of the National Library of Ireland in 1940.

Born in Abbeyfeale in 1902, Richard Hayes was the son and namesake of a bank official and amateur jockey. Much of his early life was spent in Claremorris, where his father managed the National Bank. His Clongowes Wood career was distinguished by his being in the first three places nationally in all six subjects in both the Intermediate and Leaving Certificate examinations. Moving on to Trinity College, Dublin, this gifted young man won medals for mathematics, in addition to taking three honours degrees simultaneously—Celtic Studies, Modern Languages and Philosophy. He went on to take a doctorate in law. Entering the National Library in 1924, he had risen rapidly to become its youngest-ever Director in 1940. In the meantime he had found a few spare hours in which to woo and then wed my aunt, Claire Columba Keogh, in 1928.

While I always held my mother in the highest esteem, I had my suspicions that she was the guiding influence in this unwelcome development in the tender years of her only son. At all events, she did most of the talking on matters academic, my father staying uncharacteristically silent. As indeed he might, having fled the groves of academe at 12 to get on with real life in his father's business—cattle.

Clongowes Wood, near Clane, County Kildare, had been a secondary school for boys, run by the Society of Jesus (Jesuits or 'Jays') since they had acquired it as Castle Browne from General Michael Browne as long ago as 1814. Originally a three-storey house, this forbidding edifice had been rebuilt as a Gothic Revival castle in 1788 by Thomas Wogan Browne. He had apparently acted as his own architect, which would explain a lot. Anyway, General Browne flogged his ancestral estate to the Jesuits before going off to fight in Napoleon's army.

The Jesuits had actually been suppressed by Pope Clement XIV in 1773. They got a bit of their own back when that pontiff turned up his toes a year later. However, the 'Soldiers of Christ', as they fancied themselves, remained outside the fold until Pope Pius VII relented in

1814. No sooner had he done so than Father Peter Kenny S.J. bought the castle and grounds in which to establish the Collegium Maximum for Ireland, allegedly aided and abetted by a certain Edmund Ignatius Rice, founder of the Christian Brothers. It was an unholy alliance. Kenny began enrolling scholars in May 1814, bringing the numbers up to 250 within four years. Ominously, an outbreak of fever, attributed to overcrowding, led to rapid building of extensions.

Luckily, I knew nothing of this, not that I would have much cared anyway. Life for a ten-year-old in a wartime Jesuit boarding school posed infinitely more pressing problems. Not the least of those was the ever-present threat of corporal punishment, administered with equal gusto by Jays and senior boys alike. What did become abundantly clear was the Jesuits' preference for the offspring of the professional classes, destined to become doctors, dentists, lawyers, accountants, bankers and suchlike. A cattle dealer's son from Lindsay Road, Glasnevin, simply did not fit the mould.

Nor did the cattle dealer's son from Glasnevin identify in any way whatsoever with the Jesuits' repeated calls for vocations. These were given added impetus during my time in Clongowes by the swelling movement to achieve beatification for a former inmate—Fr John Sullivan S. J. Born in Dublin in 1861, John Sullivan was the son of barrister Edward Sullivan, destined to become Lord

Chancellor of Ireland. Edward Sullivan was, of course, Church of Ireland, whereas Elizabeth, his wife, was a Catholic landowner's daughter from County Cork. Raised in his father's faith, John was sent to Portora Royal, Enniskillen, as Oscar Wilde had been. His education was completed in Trinity College, Dublin, where he was awarded the Gold Medal in Classics in 1885.

His father's death that year determined John Sullivan to uphold the family's legal tradition. Comfortably off through his inheritance, John Sullivan soon became known as the best-dressed young man in Dublin, a sports enthusiast who delighted in long walks both here and abroad. Perhaps inspired by family friend Fr Tom Finlay S.J., John caused widespread surprise when converting to Catholicism in 1896. Four years later he entered the Jesuit seminary in Tullabeg, near Tullamore, continuing his philosophy study at Stoneyhurst College, Lancashire. Once ordained in 1907 Fr Sullivan joined the Jesuit community in Clongowes, remaining there until his death in 1933. From the outset his holiness and devotion to God marked him apart, so much so that in his lifetime many began to attribute nigh-miraculous cures to his piety and powers of healing. Ever since people have made his tomb in Gardiner Street, Dublin, a place of pilgrimage, many seeking to be blessed with his vow crucifix. The campaign for his canonization continues.

Only years later did I learn of another misfit—like myself—to pass through Clongowes Wood. His name was James Augustine Aloysius Joyce and he had died in January 1941, months before I followed in his footsteps down the long avenue flanked by lime trees. Although already famous—or infamous—as an author, James Joyce was *persona non grata* in Clongowes Wood in my time there. Ironically, the regime had great tame for another alumnus, Oliver St John Gogarty, whom Joyce had portrayed as Buck Mulligan in his banned book—*Ulysses*.

CHAPTER FIVE
Second World War

L ife is full of ironies, or so hindsight makes it appear. Apropos the cattle business in Ireland, it strikes me as ironic indeed that the British should have devastated our national herd by the imposition of tariffs in 1932, only to reach out for Irish beef to feed its people less than a decade later. While that *New York Times* correspondent assigned to cover the Irish general election in that year may have been fanciful in drawing his comparison between the demagoguery of Eamon de Valera and that of Adolf Hitler, time might be said to have lent credence to his view.

True or not, the onset of the Second World War brought about an urgent, if disciplined demand for Irish beef. Actually, that demand had never completely dried up, an opportunity exploited by the Crowley brothers of Roscrea—Con Crowley and his brother Gerry. Together with German entrepreneur 'Big George' Fasenfeld they had opened Ireland's first meat factory—Roscrea Meats— when the Economic War was still waging. Although the tariff had crippled the livestock trade with England, no such tariffs or duties applied to canned meat.

By the time Roscrea Meats came on stream cows were

worth less than the £6 tariff per head. They were effectively unsaleable, turned loose by despairing farmers to forage for food wherever they might find any. Joe Ward, whose lifetime in the cattle business was so vividly related in *Strong Farmer*, described seeing a huge cow in the west of Ireland sold for just two shillings and sixpence. The seller promptly handed the half-crown to the astonished purchaser, saying that he had never given back less as a 'luck penny' and was not going to depart from that practice, whatever the circumstances.

The Crowleys and George Fasenfeld needed no second bidding. All over Ireland their agents were dispatched to buy up unwanted cows and ship them to Roscrea where they were promptly canned as 'Casserole' and shipped across the Irish Sea—tariff and duty free. Trade was not confined to Britain either. George Fasenfeld's son and namesake recalls coming across old front-page images of freighters being loaded in Irish ports, flying two flags, the tricolour and the swastika. Britain might be hungry, but Nazi Germany was starving.

While it seems incredible now, that Fianna Fáil government was so hellbent on reducing the national herd that it brought in an 'incentive scheme'. This 'scheme' was simplicity in itself. If a farmer would agree to destroying a calf, rather than rearing it, he or she would receive a bounty of £2—more than the market value of the doomed animal. Welcome as the bounty might have been in those impecunious circumstances, this 'blood money' was anathema to the national psyche. It was akin to being bribed to begin eating horsemeat. All too often the unfortunate calves were simply turned loose, to live or to die, just as those old and worthless cows had been.

My father's survival during those lean, depressed years was underpinned to a most welcome degree by his weekly contract to supply 150 head of finished bullocks to Boothman & Kaplan of Birkenhead. Kaplan would cross over on the early boat, do his business with my father, source a further 450 head from other stallholders and return by boat that same evening. Steady if unspectacular, it allowed my father to accumulate what would be considered a small fortune in today's currency, safely stashed against unforeseen contingencies in the Royal Bank, later to form part of AIB.

Oliver St John Gogarty, referred to earlier as one of Clongowes' more cherished alumni, had by this time become a member of the Irish senate. No friend of Eamon de Valera, Gogarty lost no opportunity to denounce him from the floor of the Upper House:

'I do not often make suggestions and up to this I have not been asked to advise His Holiness; but if he is ever thinking of giving titular honours to our President, he could call him not inappropriately 'The Prince of Denmark', for he is as hurling-worded and overwhelmed as Hamlet, and he has done more for the Danish market and the prosperity of Denmark than the royal family thereof.

'Instead of seizing the opportunity of Plenty, like a fanatical edition of St Francis, he is wed to his Lady Poverty—by proxy, of course—while we, who are hard set enough to live, are to tighten our belts. This sixpenny Savanarola, in a world of Woolworths, invited the nation deliberately to choose poverty which he promised in his election confidence trick to prevent: there will be food for all from the unsaleable property of other Irishmen. Already they say in Clare that the blacksmiths are shoeing the cattle so that they may gallop round the fairs on the look-out for a purchaser.

'To be consistent the potato introduced by Raleigh should be extradited and smoking taxed as a foreign game . . .

'A statesman who has no regard for the conditions of which a country's existence in the realm of Reality depends, let me say a patriot, but carried out his own policy whether it be an idea or an ideal, regardless of the present needs of the people, comes to be indistinguishable in historical results from, and confused in the memory of the citizens with, a traitor, as the saying goes, "In the pay of England".

'Therefore, I tell you to have a care, President de Valera, lest your silhouette may come to be regarded as the most sinister which ever darkened the light in genial Ireland and that it may not be without ominous significance that, during the election, your name was written on the dead walls and roofless ruins of this, our Country.'

Having prorogued the Upper House in 1936, President de Valera concluded the Economic War by means of an agreed once-off payment in lieu of the land annuities, besides securing the return of the strategic ports still occupied by the British, to Winston Churchill's fury. Out of office and out of favour, Churchill was almost a lone voice in urging the British people to prepare to take up arms against Nazi Germany.

When what Churchill had long declared inevitable duly came to pass, the Irish Free State proclaimed its neutrality. As such, it could not permit the British navy to reoccupy the ports it so desperately needed to protect the merchant shipping which now became Britain's lifeline. Perhaps unsurprisingly, the British deemed Free State needs of essential supplies lowest priority. Petrol scarcity rapidly put Ireland's motorcars off the roads for the duration. However, there were exceptions.

Busier than he had been for years, Jack Keogh telegraphed Kieran Phelan, his agent in Kilkenny, to meet him off the train at Gowran. Kieran Phelan owned 600 acres nearby, on which he finished store cattle—both grass-fed and stall-fed—of which Jack Keogh had first choice. To my father's surprise, Kieran Phelan ushered him out to a gleaming new Austin motorcar, indicated that he get in.

'What is this all about? Nobody can get any petrol.'

'It's a fact, boss. That's why I've bought you this licensed taxi. You can get all the petrol you want!'

And so Kieran Phelan and my father covered the fairs and the farms all over the southeast for the duration of 'The Emergency', as the Second World War quickly became known throughout our Irish Free State.

Kieran Phelan was one of a network of agents—Peter Roe of Roscrea another—informally contracted to my father throughout Leinster and Munster. He seldom ventured into Connaught, for cattle were rarely brought to their 'finished' state (fit for slaughter) on the lime-free lands beyond the Shannon. However, the western counties—then as now—served as a nursery for younger cattle, traditionally bought on site and shipped to Meath, Kildare and Dublin for fattening on the summer grass. Nor did my father venture into Ulster, a separate entity with its largely internal, self-contained economy.

The First World War had been a bonanza for Irish farmers, so much so that one commentator would later write: 'the last seven years of the union with Great Britain became the most prosperous years that had been experienced in modern Irish history.' Indeed, as its successor drew inexorably nearer, a 1937 article in *Ireland Today* had described the attitude of Irish farmers as they anticipated the resumption of conflict in Europe as one of 'quiet optimism.' It was not to work out quite like that.

British rationing together with a strict price-control

mechanism kept prices steady, even below pre-war prices, for some goods. Farmers made little profit from livestock exports to Britain. Then came an outbreak of the dreaded foot-and-mouth disease in 1941, with its consequent ban on the movement of livestock, the destruction of diseased animals and an embargo on the export of live cattle. Ireland was no stranger to this dreaded epidemic. As long ago as 1129 the Annals of Tigernach recorded an outbreak of 'máelgarb' which caused the death of almost all the cattle and pigs of Ireland. Controls being less draconian in those days, it persisted throughout the northern half of the country into the following year. Early Irish farming historian Fergus Kelly's research suggested 'máelgarb' as an ancient equivalent of foot-and-mouth, its symptoms including blisters on the tongue, lips, udder, teats and feet.

My father proved lighter on his feet than his competitors, if not by much. Hearing of a disused abattoir on the outskirts of Wexford town, he put that taxi to good use, getting down there as fast as he could to sign a lease of the premises. Twenty-four hours later a rival in a far bigger way of business arrived, only learning to his chagrin that he had been beaten to the punch by Jack Keogh. There being no embargo on the shipment of carcase meat, my father chartered what shipping was available to run the gauntlet of U-boats and floating mines to send those carcases, preserved with ice, to McCrackens, eager wholesalers in Birkenhead.

This piece of quick thinking made my father enough money to buy two farms in County Dublin. From the Wilkinsons he bought Powerstown, Clonee, 250 acres that he had previously been renting. Indeed, my father might be said to have made his mark there already. On that same farm the Irish Army had slaughtered 150 cattle infected with foot-and-mouth. Once they had been interred in pits and covered with quicklime, Powerstown was once again certified free to carry livestock. Rosetown, an out-farm of similar acreage in Dunshaughlin, my father bought from the McDermotts.

For all his 450 acres, my father was no more than a modest landowner in a vicinity where the Brutons farmed 3,000 acres, Pat Rooney 1,200, the Molloys 1,000 and Johnny Duffy 500. To those I should add the Leonards of Culmullen, John Mangan of Tobergreghan, the Bakers of Malahow, Kellys of Greenogue, Dick Ball of the Naul, Rogers of Ratoath and the Dreapers—Tom and Dick— of Kilsallaghan. However, that Fianna Fáil slogan—'The bullock for the road; the land for the people'—had not gone away, as Jack Keogh was to discover.

CHAPTER SIX
James Dillon

Nobody enjoys telling a story more than I do. I've even been known to tell an odd one against myself. So I imagined putting those stories on paper would be similarly enjoyable. God help me. The difference is like night and day. The spoken word wafts away into the air almost as soon as it has been uttered. And if some pedant should attempt to throw your words back in your face, you can always deny having ever said them. With the written word there can be no such escape.

> *The Moving Finger writes; and, having writ,*
> *Moves on: nor all thy Piety nor Wit*
> *Shall lure it back to cancel half a Line,*
> *Nor all thy Tears wash out a Word of it.*

This is my roundabout way of introducing a colossus in my working life—James Dillon, Minister for Agriculture 1948-1951 and again in 1954-1957. Ministers come and ministers go. That was always the way of our world. But James Dillon was different. He left his mark on the agricultural bedrock of the Irish economy. He was an extraordinary man; ahead of his time and a dinosaur.

When James Dillon entered Dáil Éireann in 1932 as

an independent deputy for Donegal he constituted an anomaly in Irish politics of that time when political affiliations still divided along civil war lines. James Dillon's political heritage went way back before 1916 and then events that followed from the Easter Rising and its inflammatory aftermath. Though he was born in 1902, his family's political connections went back three generations; to 1812 when Luke Dillon, his grandfather was forced to surrender his small-holding outside Ballaghaderreen and move into that Roscommon town, where his son Thomas opened a grocer shop. The business prospered sufficiently for Thomas to send his son, John Blake Dillon to Trinity College, where he became friends with Thomas Davis. They went on to found the Young Ireland movement.

John Dillon—John Blake Dillon's son—upheld the family's political connection, becoming an ally of Charles Stewart Parnell, whom he briefly succeeded as leader of the Irish Parliamentary Party, before standing down in favour of John Redmond. John Dillon concentrated his efforts behind the Land League movement and its Plan of Campaign, which saw him serve several terms in prison. And all the while the family business back in Ballaghaderreen grew and grew, trading by then as Monica Duff, named after Thomas Dillon's widowed sister, to whom he left it. No longer just retailers, Monica Duff & Co. diversified into haberdashery, ironmongery, bakery, tobacco, alcohol and soft drinks manufacture, seeds and fertilizers, eventually selling its own Monduff branded goods. What had started as a very modest grocery shop had become the biggest employer in the region.

By the time John Dillon died in 1927 his political legacy was already secure in the form of his younger son James. Educated at Mount St Benedict in Gorey, University College Dublin and King's Inns, James had also studied business management—a natural field for one of his merchant upbringing—both with Selfridges in London and Marshall Field in Chicago. James Dillon brought a wealth and variety of cosmopolitan experience into the distinctly parochial medium that was then Irish politics. Above and beyond the sectarian bitterness of civil war politics, James Dillon determined to carry on his inherited legacy to better the lot of Irish farmers. When the inter-party government took office in 1948 James Dillon was the automatic choice as Minister for Agriculture. A man of vision, he was already a controversial figure, with his trademark homburg hats and undertaker's suits. He alone had campaigned for the Irish Free State to take up arms against the Nazi threat in 1939, arguing that it was every right-thinking Irishman's duty to join that struggle against evil. That the Irish navy comprised one armed trawler and one former British gunboat, while the Air Corps could muster six slow-flying Lysanders and three obsolete Gloucester Gladiator fighter biplanes mattered not. It was the principle of the thing.

Even Winston Churchill—to whom Dillon was frequently likened, although he claimed that Theodore Roosevelt was his role model—latterly conceded that de Valera's neutral Irish Free State was more of a help to the Allies as such than it could ever have been as a protagonist. Not that such nuances troubled James Dillon any more than did his expulsion from the Fine Gael party for his warmongering pronouncements. By then he had transferred from Donegal to Monaghan, where he was automatically returned in every election until his retirement from active political life in 1965. He actually retired as leader of the Fine Gael party, which had long since welcomed him back to its fold.

When James Dillon was appointed minister for Agriculture he was acutely aware of the dire state into which farming had regressed as a direct consequence of that calamitous Economic War of the 1930s. As stock had plummeted in value, so had thousands of acres of good land been allowed to revert to a mixture of scrub and semi-marsh, starved for decades of fertilizer. Rejoicing in the news that the Irish Free State was to be included in the American Marshall Aid plan to the tune of $128m in loans and $18m in grant aid, lest the country begin to court communism, Dillon moved to bag the lot for agricultural revival, primarily land reclamation. It had come to his knowledge that the national beef herd was suffering from asphosphoris, a disease caused by lack of phosphates in the herbage.

Advised by G.A. Holmes, on lines already proven successful in New Zealand, the Minister made grassland his priority. A nationwide scheme of land drainage was to be followed by soil testing to ascertain the required dosage of lime and fertilizers. In response to criticism from Fianna Fáil deputies that such measures would merely ensure that non-viable farms would simply be perpetuated, the Minister retorted that it was surely preferable that small farmers should become self-supporting rather than become a burden on society as a whole. Apropos soil testing, the Minister regaled the Dáil with his earlier experiences of land analysis under a Fianna Fáil regime. 'I remember going down to the Agricultural College in Ballyhaise in County Cavan, where I found an old man and a boy testing soil samples by a remarkable method. They had rigged up a bicycle wheel, with a medicine bottle tied to it, in which the soil sample was mixed with water. The boy turned the bicycle wheel, and thus the soil was tested. This was representative of the state of affairs at that time.'

In 1949 James Dillon moved his Land Bill in the Dáil. He aimed to reclaim 4.5 million acres, for which the state would proved two-thirds of the cost up to a maximum of £20 per acre. But there was a proviso. Should the soil still be below par after reclamation work was complete, then a portion

JOHN 'JACK' KEOGH (1902–1976)
—to whose memory Cattleman is dedicated.

LOAN FOR CONSTRUCTION OF NEW CATTLE MARKET,
NORTH CIRCULAR ROAD, DUBLIN.

No. *96*

Received from *Messrs Duffy, Mangan & Butler* the sum of *One Hundred* pounds, sterling, being the amount of the *fifth* instalment of £20 per cent. upon the sum of *Five Hundred* sterling, which he has agreed to lend to the Right Honorable the Lord Mayor, Aldermen, and Burgesses of Dublin, part of the sum of £20,000, agreed to be raised by them for construction of a New Cattle Market, on the North Circular road, between Aughrim-street and Prussia-street, in the City of Dublin. Said sum of £*500* sterling, *being* paid up in full, to be secured by one or more mortgage or mortgages under their Corporate Seal, charged upon the Improvement Fund of the Borough of Dublin, and to be payable *twenty* years after the date from the 29th day of September, 1863, with interest at the rate of £6 per centum per annum. Such mortgage or mortgages to be delivered to said *Messrs Duffy, Mangan & Butler* upon his paying up the said full sum of £*500* sterling, and signing an agreement indorsed upon each such mortgage, that in case the net amount of tolls, fees, and other legal income of said Market, shall, after deducting the amount of rent, rates, taxes, repairs, salaries, expenses of management, and other necessary outgoings of said Market, be not sufficient to pay interest upon the entire sum borrowed for the above purpose, at the said rate of £6 per cent. per annum, that they the said *Messrs Duffy, Mangan & Butler* *his* executors, administrators, or assigns, or the future holders of such mortgages, will, in such latter case, accept such lower rate of interest, as the said net amount of income of said Market will be adequate to pay, on the said entire sum to be so borrowed—the said sum now deposited to bear interest at 6 per cent. from this date, save as aforesaid.

Dated this *13* day of *October* 1863.

Louis Coakline

Treasurer of the City of Dublin.

The financing of the Dublin Cattle Market

The Author. I never was camera-shy.

Then we were four (L to R) Christina, Marie, Gertrude and Raymond Keogh

*1948—making my debut with the Ward Union Staghounds,
an association that was to last for 55 years*

Elizabeth 'Sisi' Empress of Austria (1837–1898) (BY C. DE GRIMM FOR VANITY FAIR)

William George 'Bay' Middleton (1846–1892) (FROM VANITY FAIR 1883)

Leonard Morrogh—Master of the Wards, dubbed the 'Nimrod of Ireland'.

*Standish Collen, joint–master, with his wife
at a meet of the Ward Union in the 1960s*

Percy Maynard (centre) with the Ward Union at Ratoath Manor

*The opening meet, Ashbourne, 1964 (*PHOTO C.C. FENNELL*)*

Mrs Philip O'Connor and hostess Joan Keogh at whose home in Finnstown 600 enjoyed the annual Hunt Ball

Toddy O'Sullivan (left) and Kenneth O'Reilly–Hyland at a meet

Powerstown, home from 1951 to 1965

Phoenix Park races in the 1950s, (L to R) Eileen Nolan and Joan Keogh

Family Keogh—(L to R) Dominic, Sara, Simon, Joan and Raymond, Rachel

of the grant would be paid not in cash but in limestone and phosphates. In answer to his opposition critics who contended that such assistance should be free to the farmers taking part, the Minister had this to say in characteristic orotund fashion. 'Our people are not sycophantic paupers who can be bought by shovelling public money into their hands ... the role of the State is to make available the means of doing that which the owner of the land has never been able to do since his father bought it from the landlord, and which he would never be able to do if the community as a whole are not prepared to make provision for doing it.'

It can hardly have been coincidental that the pilot scheme was initiated in Mayo on 16 August 1949, the 70th anniversary to the very day of Michael Davitt's founding of the Land League in Castlebar. The minister would also use Mayo as the trial ground for his preposterous advertising campaigns aimed at upgrading the county's fowl population. One such read: GALLINA SENESCENS DELENDA EST. Criticized by the opposition for his shameless gimmickry, the Minister stated that he relied upon his readers' natural curiosity to prompt them to ask the local clergy to translate from the Latin. Those who did were intrigued to learn that the Minister for Agriculture had taken newspaper space to advise them that 'the ageing hen must be destroyed'. His intention was that those laid-out hens be replaced by chickens. For decades to come they would be referred to in Gaeltacht areas as 'Dillon's bheaga' (little Dillons).

Fianna Fáil lost no opportunity to vilify the most ambitious, reforming Minister for Agriculture since the foundation of the state. 'One of the greatest afflictions since Cromwell . . . a rancher deliberately turning this country into a large grazing ranch for the purpose of producing cheaper food for England.' That was no more than a twist on a much earlier Fianna Fáil war cry: 'The bullock for the road, the land for the people.' The Minister had an answer for his critics, as he always had. Cattle exports had increased from £15.6m in 1947 to £22.7m in 1950. During the corresponding period poultry exports had risen from £1.9m to £3.9m and eggs from £1.6m to £5.1m. '*Gallina senescens delenda est*'—how are ye!

Never happier than when baiting the opposition in the Dáil, Minister Dillon told the house that the day of the farm horse was well and truly over, and that tractors were the key to progressive farming. While his opponents branded the Minister a traitor to Ireland's horse breeding industry, the Minister replied that, whereas industrial workers were assured of having the most modern technology at their disposal, the unfortunate farm workers relied on machinery seventy years out of date.

James Dillon saw the state's role in agriculture as one of stimulating productivity, not of obtrusive intervention. 'I am in favour of letting my neighbour run his farm his own way; but if he wants my opinion on the best dairy cow he can keep in this country it must be the dual purpose shorthorn cow.

'I know there are a lot of old maids and cranks in this country who keep Jerseys and Guernseys and Friesians . . . and they are out in the morning brushing them down and washing them with soap and water and feeding them with milk and stuffing them with little handfuls of grass and treating them as if they were Pekinese dogs. The poor old shorthorn comes in and is milked and gets a slap on the behind and is sent out on the hill for the rest of the evening.

'Her lactation is then compared with the lactation of the Friesian, who is fed nearly with rashers each morning . . . Then the Friesian is produced at the Royal Dublin Society Show and her milk is flooding the whole place and they are running for buckets to collect it and take it off.

'Then you find that the butter fat content is 1.4 and you begin to wonder if this is the water to wash the dairy with or milk from the cow. The poor old shorthorn comes in from the side of the hill and she is milked and out she goes again; she comes in again in the evening and she is milked and there is no respect for her at all.'

Patrick Smith TD, James Dillon's predecessor as Minister for Agriculture in the Fianna Fáil government was apoplectic, calling Dillon 'a shorthorn fool who will wreck everything . . . his greatest codology—the double dairy cow, the single dairy cow and the beef shorthorn bull, crossing one with the other and expecting to retain milk here and beef there.'

Smith always insisted that the Minister had dubbed him a 'calf jobber's son', an accusation that Dillon adamantly denied. However, this lifelong cinema buff he did confide to one of his aides that he could never be too hard on Paddy Smith—'He's so like Spencer Tracy.'

Misguided as he was in his reliance upon the shorthorn as the economic saviour of the Irish beef and dairy economy, James Dillon had attained a degree of popularity as a progressive and enlightened Minister for Agriculture that his cabinet colleagues could only admire, even envy. As it was, dissension within the ranks of that inter-party government provoked a general election in 1951. Entertaining as he invariably was in the Dáil, James Dillon came into his own on the hustings, where he openly invited heckling among his audience. On one such occasion at a rally in O'Connell Street he adjured his listeners to heed the dissenters in their midst. 'You hear that low moaning sound . . . the voice of the ghosts of Mr de Valera's slaughtered calves.' We Irish may sometimes forgive, but we never forget.

Now it was Fianna Fáil's turn once again. Their budget of 2 April 1952 was so severe as to send unemployment soaring to 90,000, leading to demonstrations by civil servants and unemployed alike. One such devolved into a riot in which over seventy people were injured. One commentator gave it as his view that the severity of that budget 'probably contributed to both the reality and the atmosphere of depression ... the relentless pursuit of deflation in 1953 and 1954 further accentuated the slump . . . This deflationary crusade discouraged investment in manufacturing industry and may have inhibited export development.'

The beleaguered electorate turned back to a Fine Gael-dominated coalition in 1954, in which James Dillon became Minister for Agriculture for a second time. Ironically, the success of his first term now turned upon him, for the massive increase in beef exports led to a domestic price rise of 7d per pound for beef. Moreover, the release of the most recent census figures revealed the lowest population ever recorded in Ireland's history. Under John A. Costello the government responded with a National Plan for economic recovery, unveiled in October 1956. Dillon's influence became clearer yet when it became known that this recovery was to be spearheaded by agriculture. £1m had been earmarked for a nationwide scheme to eradicate bovine tuberculosis. Short-term credit facilities were to be made available to small and medium-sized farmers. Stable prices would be set for beef, wheat, barley and Grade A pigs, a guarantee to the producers of a fair and assured return on their time and investment. As luck would have it, the Soviet invasion of Hungary, the Suez crisis and the unwelcome escalation of IRA violence north of the border ensured that Dillon's initiatives were not to be realized.

Twelve months later, now as opposition spokesman on agriculture, James Dillon gave the Dáil the benefit of his beliefs. 'I think we have to face the fact that we will never be rich in this country . . . We are primarily an agricultural economy whose natural resources consist of twelve million acres of arable land, and the people who live on it. That will never provide in terms of money and goods the same standard of living as is available in the great industrial economies.'

By now the father figure of the Fine Gael party, James Dillon was elected its leader in 1959, once again on the bandwagon to safeguard Irish agriculture. He sought: 'greater integration of the economies of Ireland and the united Kingdom . . . a reciprocal trade agreement which would give Ireland a link with their prices in respect of cattle, sheep, pigs and bacon.'

The Common Market debate of 1961 saw the old warrior at his most prescient. 'In signing this Treaty [of Rome] we authorize the authorities in Brussels to tell us in respect of certain matters what Oireachtas Éireann may and may not do. We limit our discretion in a variety of matters relating to social services, employment practices relevant to certain measures which we have heretofore employed to stimulate employment.'

However, apropos such loss of sovereignty, James Dillon TD was crystal clear in his evaluation. 'We simply cannot afford to have the tariffs on agricultural produce levied against us in the British market. Free access to the British market is vital to the agricultural industry of Ireland and the agricultural industry provides employment directly and indirectly for three-quarters of the people of Ireland. It is the foundation of our whole economic life and unless it can be made to prosper, Ireland could not provide a reasonable standard of living for her people.'

James Dillon retired from a lifetime in politics in 1965, living on until 1986, the year in which Monica Duff & Co. likewise came to the end of its commercial life. John Blake Dillon, the only child of his marriage to Maura Phelan, broke the family tradition by eschewing politics for his successful career in accountancy. Remarkably—to my way of thinking at least—it was not until the last millennium had drawn to its close that James Dillon received posthumous recognition through Maurice Manning's splendid biography to which I have made extensive recourse. I could have done no less in this attempt to pay my own modest yet heartfelt tribute to one of the political giants of my lifetime in the cattle trade.

CHAPTER SEVEN

Cutting My Teeth

The winter of 1947 is still referred to as 'the worst in living memory', albeit by a diminishing number qualified to make that claim. Lest you think it an exaggeration, snow still lay in the ditches in Roscommon in the month of May. Actually, that marked the end of a climatic catastrophe that had befallen Ireland the previous autumn. The aftermath to a truly awful, rain-sodden summer had put the harvest in jeopardy. In other circumstances, shortage of homegrown grain might have been offset by supplies from our old ally, America. But on this occasion American surplus had been allocated to feed the starving millions across post-war Europe.

The Irish Government issued a national appeal to any and all able-bodied people to volunteer to go into the countryside to help save the harvest of '46, which could only be done by hand, so sodden were the fields in which it now, for the most part, lay lodged. *The Irish Times* covered this remarkable mass exodus into what was for many the unknown. In response to the initial summons 2,000 volunteers and 600 troops left Dublin assembly centres by train, by buses provided by CIE and IAWS and army lorries to play their part. With a window in the weather it was estimated that 5,000 might suffice to make the harvest safe.

Race meetings were postponed. Greyhound trials were deferred to the evenings. Rugby matches and practice sessions were abandoned. The Department of Finance, the ESB, Dublin Corporation and Guinness were among the large employers giving their workers dispensation to participate. It paid off, as *The Irish Times* instanced. 'With the aid of farm workers, voluntary labour and troops, the 80 acres of wheat belonging to Mr J. Noonan, Clonkeen, Co Dublin, were completely threshed yesterday and taken away to the mills . . . The rations position was improving, stated Mr P. Burke, TD, of the Red Cross, yesterday, but far more help was needed.'

The seriousness of the situation became dramatically evident in February 1947 when John Charles McQuaid, Archbishop of Dublin, proclaimed an official dispensation to his flock to ignore the fasting laws, because people had become so dangerously undernourished. Such laxity on John Charles's part was not bestowed lightly.

Not, I think, that I was in need of any such dispensation. A combination of unease with the 'ambience' of my Clongowes Wood habitat and an aversion to school cuisine had consigned me to the infirmary with what was subsequently diagnosed as scarlet fever. Luckily for me, the threat of epidemic had long formed part of Clongowes folk memory. I was dispatched forthwith to the Cork Street Fever Hospital, never to return. It was—in the Jesuit canon—an instance of the end justifying the means.

When I did return to health, so I did to happiness. My father decreed that I should complete my secondary education in an infinitely more practical milieu. He sent me down to serve an informal apprenticeship with Kieran Phelan on his 600-acre farm near Gowran, County Kilkenny. As the Phelans had no family they virtually adopted me as their own. I was like a pig in the proverbial. But I was also educated in 'finished' cattle husbandry.

Kieran Phelan ran an operation that was ahead of its time in those post-war years, for he produced both grass-fed and stall-fed cattle for slaughter. He wasn't alone, of course. Johnny Greene of Kilkee was stall-feeding 3,000 head. Juan Greene, his son, having qualified as a doctor of medicine, went on to found the Irish Farmers' Association. Others to run dual operations were the Copes, the Ashmores and Fred Wright, who farmed 1,000 acres to that end. Willie Ashe of Narraghmore, besides being one of the biggest graziers in the country, also turned his hand to winter feeding.

Accustomed as I already was to simply fattening 'store' cattle on the lush summer pastures in north County Dublin, I had to learn from scratch the complexities of mixed beef farming. Kieran grew barley for both its grain and its straw, sugar beet (the tops for feeding, the beet itself for the sugar factory in Carlow), in addition to setting meadows aside for hay. It was a lot of work. But for me it was both a learning curve and a labour of love. Better, I said to myself, that any university book-learning. This was both theory and practice rolled into one.

During my contented time with the Phelans, Johnny Byrne, a friend and rival of my father's in the Dublin cattle market, got into the habit of teasing my father about his ambitions for his son and heir. My father refused to rise to the bait, saying each time that Raymond was destined to do as his father, his grandfather and his great-grandfather before him had done. It was also a quiet way of reminding Johnny that the Keoghs were a 'long-tailed' family in Ireland's biggest business. Johnny was not to be put down without a skirmish. 'Give the lad £300. Send him to the north to tangle for cattle. If he comes back with any of it left, you might be in with a chance!'

In the event, my father made a rather greater act of faith in his only son. Wearying of the endless round of country fairs, he had resolved to send me in his stead. He brought me in to the Royal Bank in Foster Place, introduced me to the manager and organized a facility for me to draw down funds to the maximum of £10,000. That was a hell of a lot of money in 1948. Not, of course, that there was any risk of that trust being misplaced . . .

Not in what was a seller's market, supplying cattle of all and any description to the European mainland, where the indigenous bovine stock had been massacred throughout the war years. My father had already established contacts for both Belgium and Holland. Omer Vanlandeghem had the contracts for Belgium, while a man by the name of Williams filled the orders for Holland.

Unfortunately, at a time when beasts were assessed by eye—in the absence of scales—this teenager's eye proved a sorry substitute for his father's. Moreover, wily farmers were not slow to put a youngster to the test. A favourite farmers' ploy when offering beasts for sale was to put up a 'matched' batch of bullocks, say fifteen in all. Of those a dozen would be up to the desired weight, the other three significantly below it. The rules of this game required the prospective buyer to express interest in the dozen that were up to the mark, only to be coaxed to bid for them as a job lot.

The buyer must stand firm, saying that only the dozen suited his order, but under no circumstances must he bid, lest offence be taken. Protocol required the vendor to put his cattle on price. Only then was the buyer allowed to propose a lower offer. When that was rejected, as custom required, the intending buyer should turn away, visibly disappointed, departing slowly enough to permit easy recapture.

At the heel of the hunt a deal would begin to materialize, facilitated by the unexplained but nigh-inevitable appearance of the tangler. He would seize both men's right hands, struggling theatrically to join them together as all the while bids, counter-bids, denials, accusations and counter-accusations filled the air. If, at length, a deal were struck, both buyer and seller must spit on his right hand before pressing the flesh to signify closure. It was all the greatest of sport, standing in a sea of cowshite, all too often in the pouring rain. No wonder my father was happy to delegate.

Trouble was, the beasts I was buying as 'finished'—to my eye—had an unfortunate habit of shedding a hundredweight or more by the time they were off-loaded at Cabra Junction, to my father's voluble dismay. It did not take Johnny Byrne long to receive this joyous intelligence. And exploit it:

'Ah hello, Jack. How's your young lad gettin' along then?'

'Getting along, is it? Sure and I had a right to send him to Oxford or Cambridge. Could hardly have been as dear.'

CHAPTER EIGHT
Barn Hall, Leixlip

My father was by his nature a most cautious man, never in any danger of, as we say, 'losing the run of himself'. He was accustomed to living and working within his own 'comfort zone'. As such he was completely taken aback by a telephone call one day in 1951 from Gerard Counihan, Turvey House, Donabate, the farm his father had acquired through opportunism in the First World War. Was Jack aware that American beef producers had gone on strike, intent on getting a better price from their produce from the giant meat processors in Chicago? Whether he knew or not, such faraway developments were of no consequence to Jack Keogh. He had his own affairs to concern him, not least the matter of teaching his son and heir how to buy cattle to turn a profit.

But Gerard was insistent. Here lay a golden opportunity to exploit another vast, unexpected, potentially unlimited market for Irish beef. What was more, the intrepid Gerry had already chartered a refrigerated ship to convey all this Irish beef across the Atlantic Ocean to voracious Yanks, who simply could not survive without steaks, steaks and more steaks. As to what was in it for Jack? Why, Jack could have 25% of the space on said ship!

In yet another instance of the Counihan cheek paying off, Gerry had caught my father on one of his very rare 'up-for-it!' days. It must have been a day on which my father's persistent depression abated sufficiently to allow him some degree of lateral thinking. And they came around only once in a blue moon, if even then.

Setting aside his doubts about what he called 'the phantom ship', Jack Keogh put together a consortium of five—himself included—to form Irish Meat Packers. The cattle were duly purchased, slaughtered in the Dublin abattoir, packed aboard the 'phantom ship', which appeared as and when Gerry Counihan had said it would and duly offloaded on to the steak-starved American market. The boys cleared a cool £60,000. Tally-ho!

At this distance in time I could not be absolutely certain that one at least did not begin to project a future for Irish Meat Packers along the lines so brilliantly executed by a butchering family from Manchester—the Vesteys. Fifty years or so previously the Vesteys had sent one of their number out to Argentina on a voyage of discovery. To his amazement and delight he had found that the Argentinians ate only the best cuts of steak and discarded the rest of the beef from their innumerable herds that grazed the pampas. Before you could say 'knife', the Vesteys had constructed their own abattoirs, purchased their own fleet of refrigerated ships, organized their own butchering plants in England, to supply their own countrywide chain of butcher shops, which they called Dewhursts. Why, they had even got around that tiresome business of paying tax to the Inland Revenue!

With their new-found wealth the boys created their very own meat factory outside Leixlip, a sleepy little village to the west of Dublin. It came into being on 200 acres in the townland called Barn Hall, for which they paid £13,000 to the estate of William P. Ronaldson. To avoid confusion it should be said that there are two Barn Halls. One contains 'The Wonderful Barn', described below. The other contained a different, more prosaic, but fit for purpose two-storeyed concrete barn, which could well have been designed for adaptation as an abattoir, which is what happened to it.

Leixlip—at the confluence of the Liffey and Rye Water rivers, takes its name form the Danish 'Lax-hlaup' meaning salmon leap. The Annals of the Four Masters record a battle between the Danes and the Leinstermen taking place at nearby Confey in 915. Victory for the Danes gave them possession of 'lax-hlaup'.

As for Barn Hall—'The Wonderful Barn'—'A remarkable conical-shaped building . . . built by one of the Conollys of Castletown, completed in 1743 . . . A flight of 94 steps winds round the exterior to the embattled turret, 73 feet above the base . . . This curious edifice . . . was probably commenced during the severe winter of 1741-2 to give employment to the poor, and the name Barn Hall, originally given to the entire establishment, has been adopted as the modern designation of the townland in which it stands.'—so defined and explained by Weston St John Joyce in his *Neighbourhood of Dublin*.

In days of yore Leixlip had been a favourite inland resort for Dubliners, its spa waters being as highly esteemed for their curative qualities as the better known spa in nearby Lucan. Constantia Maxwell borrowed this word portrait for her ever-popular *Dublin under the Georges*. 'According to a writer in Anthologia Hibernica, a gentleman who apparently had nothing else to do one day in the summer of 1794 amused himself by sitting at his window from six o'clock in the morning till five o'clock at night counting the numbers of coaches, post-chaises, jaunting cars, landaus, common cars, and people on horseback who passed on the Dublin road on their way to the spa. He estimated that (with pedestrians and vehicles from adjacent parts of the country) at least 12,000 persons must have visited Leixlip that day, attracted by the accounts that had been published of the wonderful cures effected by the waters.'

If that attendance figure sounds somewhat fantastical, a parallel account, reproduced in *Dublin—The Fair City*, by Peter Somerville-Large, is more credible. 'Among well-to-do Catholics a favourite Sunday outing was to the two famous St Catherine's Wells at Leixlip, both of which were known for their cures. In 1794 an observer counted eleven hundred people passing one day on their way to Leixlip. Four hundred and fifty travelled on horseback, while others passed in fifty-five coaches, twenty-nine post-chaises, twenty-five noddies, eighty-two jaunting cars, twenty gigs, six open landaus and two hundred and twenty-one common cars.'

Hardly had the lights come on and the processing lines begun to move in Barn Hall than the American farmers resolved their difference with the processors. The American market was no more. His partners melted away, leaving a despondent Jack Keogh to go to the Royal Bank, resigned to discharging what had become a £20,000 overdraft. In vain did the bank manager try to make Mr Keogh, a valued customer, understand that he needed only to get some good accountancy advice to ensure that the asset was now his, through his partners' default. In clearing the corporate debt he was now the legal owner of the factory with its 200 acres, free and unencumbered. It was his.

Whereas Gerry Counihan had got my father on one of his good days, the bank manager did not. Deaf to that well-meant advice, my father cleared the overdraft and simply walked away, putting that roller-coaster ride behind him. Forever, as he thought at the time. However, because he had made no effort to gather in his former partners' shareholdings, my father found himself enmeshed once again when the opportunity arose to supply the US armed forces then stationed in Europe. Suddenly, the 'sleeping' partners sprang to life, repaid Jack Keogh a portion of what he had been stuck for and rejoiced at being back in business once more, profits to be divided exactly as before. While the American forces business was the core, a contract to provide Marks & Spencer with high-specification canned meats constituted the icing on that particular cake. At the other extreme of the meat scale, the livers which failed veterinary inspection were sent elsewhere to be turned into dogfood. Waste not, want not.

Waste as a verb is one thing, waste as a noun quite another, as beleaguered Leixlip residents were soon to discover. IMP could only plead guilty to fouling the Liffey with by-products for which there was absolutely no market, principally beef stomachs. Had the demand for tripe been greater, then perhaps . . . If that were not enough, in being awarded the Department of Agriculture contract to slaughter TB reactors, IMP was subsequently accused of infecting a considerable proportion of the local populace with brucellosis, contracted by employees processing reactor carcases and then transmitted to their families.

In the early 1960s a merger took place between Irish Meat Packers, Leixlip, with Irish Prime Meats, the Grand Canal Street plant controlled by Frank Quinn. Together with Terry Kennedy, the IMP general manager, Quinn achieved a disquieting measure of executive control. Not that his partners minded much, as long as European markets continued to purchase inexhaustible volumes of chilled carcase meat and the profits rolled in. Combined turnover of the two plants reached £20m., reputedly the largest meat plant in Europe.

A balance sheet such as this was bound to attract bidders. One such to come a-courting was Cork Marts, successfully as it transpired. For £3.2m, plus a portion of the next four years' profits, the merged companies became a subsidiary of Cork Marts. Major Maurice Donegan became chairman, Jerome Beechinor chief executive and Batt Higgins financial controller. Everybody was happy, for a while.

Only when a highly speculative contract to supply meat to Israel reduced Cork Marts' recent acquisition to insolvency did the proverbial hit the fan. Some unsavoury practices came to light, notwithstanding the mysterious absence of any proper accounts. One striking discrepancy concerned the quantities of fat rendered from beasts slaughtered in Leixlip and those slaughtered in Grand Canal Street. For some strange reason the Leixlip beasts yielded zero fat, whereas their Grand Canal Street counterparts yielded twice the fat that might be considered normal. It then transpired that Frank Quinn was surreptitiously transferring £3,000-worth of fat each week from Leixlip to his own original plant to boost the latter's balance sheet. Was it fraud? Was it theft? Is there any difference?

Cork Marts appealed for government intervention to save the two plants, successfully, to the tune of £2m. Actually, such assistance was not as bizarre as it might at first appear. It could be argued that every beast that left Ireland on the hoof took with it five viable jobs directly related to the killing, dismemberment, processing and tanning of those animals butchered in this country. In this instance the combined payroll in both plants ran into many hundreds.

Eventually Cork Marts closed down both plants, dissolving the company formed on their purchase. The vacuum thus created was speedily filled by such as Larry Goodman's Anglo-Irish Meats, Bernard Allen's Drogheda plant, Keepak in Clonee and Roscommon and various others. The Leixlip site eventually became home to Hewlett Packard.

CHAPTER NINE

Carrick Byrn

My father, who had married into 114 Lindsey Road all those years ago and reared his family there, never had any intention of living elsewhere. Well, if he had, he kept all such thoughts to himself, being that sort of man. However, depression can do strange things to its sufferers—more numerous than is generally imagined—and this was probably an instance of a sufferer's mind being triggered by the unexpected.

One Sunday in 1954, shortly after I had gone to live in the modern Georgian-style house built on the Powerstown farm, my father asked John Kennedy to take him for a drive.

'Anywhere in particular you'd like to go, Jack?'

Ah, would we give the southside a look over? I was hardly ever down that way.'

Their wanderings took them to Brighton Road, Foxrock—already a 'very good address', though nothing like as densely populated—where my father's eye was drawn to a 'For Sale' sign, outside a house in its own spacious gardens by the name of Carrick Byrn. They stopped to have a closer look. The gardens must have been at their best, for the riot of colour lifted my father's spirits 'This place would do my heart good, John. If it can be bought any way right, it's mine.'

That extraordinary impulse must have been triggered by the Carrick Byrn garden, in all its summer glory. Just what reactions gardens can produce was brought to mind by the passing of Ambrose Congreve, creator of that amazing garden in Mount Congreve. He died, appropriately, at the Chelsea Flower Show, having recently turned 104. At his centenary lunch in 2007 Ambrose cited an ancient proverb.

> *To be happy for an hour, have a glass of wine.*
> *To be happy for a day, read a book.*
> *To be happy for a week, take a wife.*
> *To be happy forever, make a garden.*

Carrick Byrn belonged to a recently deceased member of the Jacob family, whose executors had entrusted its sale to the 'Rat' Hamilton, an auctioneer in Molesworth Street. How Willoughby Hamilton came to be known as 'Rat' is a mystery, but he had clearly come to terms with that unattractive nickname, for he apparently signed his cheques Rat Hamilton. Perhaps it ran in the family. His uncle and namesake became the first and only Irishman ever to become Wimbledon champion when successful in 1890. He was known as 'Ghost' Hamilton. 'Rat' topped the world badminton ratings in the 1930s.

While neither tennis nor badminton were hobbies of mine, perhaps I missed out, if Sigmund Freud is to be believed. In 1923 the bould Sigmund wrote: 'All the cultural achievements of which man is so proud, all his spiritual values and the like, are merely sublimations of basic instinctual drives, sex and tennis being the most fundamental.'

Anyway! My father put Brendan Brophy in to bid on his behalf at the auction. But Brendan's bid of £8,200 was deemed insufficient. The property was withdrawn from the market. Disappointed at missing out on what he now perceived to be a bargain, my father took himself across to the Hibernian Hotel, seeking solace in the basement Buttery Bar, where Jack or George—past masters, both, of the short measure—ensured his whiskey tumbler was never less than half full. Jack and George were always reputed to have been in the pay of British intelligence throughout the 'Emergency'. They were certainly very well placed if that were the case.

Having let the hare sit till the brown dog could kill it, my father instructed Brendan to sound out the 'Rat' Hamilton again. Yes, Brendan might reveal the intending purchaser's identity if he thought fit. He did. The 'Rat' duly invited Mr Keogh to call upon him at his Molesworth Street premises. The 'Rat' advised his would-be buyer that the executors sought an advance upon the £8,200. my father was thus being asked to bid against himself—anathema to a dealing man.

'Mr Hamilton, there's £8,200 on the table, a very fair price. I can get the money immediately, or I can go down the country with it tomorrow to buy cattle. And if that's what I do do, then there'll be no £8,000, nor even the colour of it.'

The 'Rat' did not hesitate. 'Mr Keogh, the property is yours. Congratulations! Very well bought, if I may say. And I wish you every happiness with it.'

'Well, well,' my father replied. 'Is that a fact? Well, let it be lucky, for me and all belonging to me!'

Only as my father was heading off to his solicitor to progress the transaction did the 'Rat' Hamilton beckon him back. 'Was there something else, Mr Hamilton?'

'Well, yes. Mr Keogh. There is something else you may not know about. It's that 10-acre field behind Carrick Byrn. You've bought that too. It forms part of the property.'

Ten acres is ten acres, wherever it may be located, good for so many beasts to the acre, depending on the land, of course. And so it came to pass that the denizens of Brighton Road, Foxrock, all-too-soon became familiar with the lowing of cattle, a forgotten sound, banished long since from their leafy, suburban Arcadia. Consternation quickly gave way to widespread fears of a collapse in property values throughout that select neighbourhood. You could, I suppose, liken the collective reaction to the sudden appearance of immigrants from very hot countries as the people next door. However, as all this took place in 1954, the analogy does not really hold good, for the simple reason that people from hot countries had not made their way to this isle of saints and scholars. Nor would they do so for a further fifty years.

Those startled neighbours included Jack Cavey, Jaguar agent, wool broker John Joyce and financier Jack McCann, married to a sister of Tom Roche of Cement-Roadstone and subsequently developer of the West Link bridge, that money spinner which spans the Liffey as part of the M50.

For whatever reason, my father eventually relented. The cattle departed Brighton Road, never to return. Instead, he rented the ten-acre field to J.A. Keogh, an unrelated namesake, to graze horses, thoroughbreds, they were. That practice continued long after his death. Gertie, my sister, used to keep an eye on Mr Keogh's broodmares, for that is mostly what they were.

Going out on her regular morning tour of inspection in 1996 Gertie discovered that Aberedw, one of the mares, had foaled down overnight and was now proudly suckling a colt foal by Montelimar. Bred as he was, the youngster did not see a racecourse until he had turned five years of age, when he finished second in his first four outings for trainer Willie Mullins and owner Niall F. Quaid. The following year he got the hang of things, winning at Clonmel by 20 lengths. In 2003 he began to show where his talents really lay when winning the Grand National Trial Chase at Punchestown, ridden by young Sam Curling, the artist's son.

By the time he had justified favouritism in the 2004 Thyestes Chase at Gowran Park he carried the colours of Trevor Hemmings, the wealthy Liverpudlian whose dearest wish it was to win the Grand National on his local course. He came close too, only to find the final obstacle just one fence too far. There was always next year . . . Trained with that one objective, he showed his wellbeing when winning his prep race at Fairyhouse in February.

They sent him off favourite for the 2005 Grand National with Ruby Walsh on board. And this time the hard luck story belonged to another as Hedgehunter galloped resolutely to the line, realizing the lifetime dream of his owner, who had begun his working life in Britain as a bricklayer's apprentice, putting himself through night school to become one of the wealthier men in that country.

Carrick Byrn's 10-acre field had proved good to one Keogh. How many Grand National winners have first seen the light of day in Foxrock? It could have done likewise for other Keoghs. When their mother died, Gertie, Christina and Marie—all of them married with their own families—decided to dispose of Carrick Byrn. Years later, at the height of the Irish propery boom—as the Celtic Tiger roared defiance at all nay-sayers—that 10-acre field made €50 million.

CHAPTER TEN

Livestock Credit Corporation

Every cloud, they say, has a silver lining. In my father's case his travails with Irish Meat Packers was the genesis of his finest achievement, the creation of the Livestock Credit Corporation in 1958. At the time IMP was contracted to supply beef from 1,000 high quality, finished bullocks to the US armed forces in Europe—in January. Traditionally farmers would not sell cattle in January. In an effort to overcome that age-old reluctance, my father canvassed major stall-feeders in October, offering a guaranteed price of £7 per hundredweight, payable on delivery of said beasts for slaughter in January.

The biggest of those—Johnny Greene of Athy—demurred, convinced as he was that he would get marginally more for his stock in the spring. However, Jim Ashmore and the Copes agreed to contract for supply on the basis of the proffered guarantee. Willie Browne was another prepared to sign up. He had the facilities. He had the fodder. But his bank manager would not advance the money required to purchase the required 600 bullocks, at approximately £50 per head. My father suggested that Willie leave that problem to him.

Thus did my father and I pay a visit to Jim Bastow, partner in Bastow Charlton, Accountants, and the leading player in international beef credit guarantees. Briefly, that was the well-established system whereby a bank—essentially the Royal Bank—paid the vendor when he consigned his processed cattle, collecting from the buyer when he received the goods some time later. Having explained his scheme for buying the necessary store cattle and 'warehousing' them for finishing with various credit-strapped farmers, my father was asked what facility he had in mind. When he mentioned £20,000, Jim Bastow immediately responded by asking whether his firm could take a financial interest in this venture to the tune of £5,000. That was exactly the form of endorsement and encouragement Jack Keogh sought as reassurance. The respect was in fact mutual, built up over years of successful cooperation.

Confirmed now in the wisdom of this project, my father suggested Jim Bastow approach the Royal Bank for a facility of £50,000. Jim Bastow instead asked for—and got—facilities to the tune of £250,000, unsecured and with no personal guarantees. Nobody else had sufficient power and influence to broker such a deal. Thus did the Livestock Credit Corporation come into being. It was unique as a credit source for farmers in that it made finance available for livestock. Other institutions were prepared to finance plant, machinery, additional land, but invariably demanding the deeds of the farm in question as security. Livestock they simply would not touch. Too uncertain. The brutes might fail to thrive, contract disease, perhaps even die.

Price fluctuations were another cause for bankers' reluctance to lend. Not that Johnny Greene needed bank finance for his stall-fed cattle. But this was one instance in which his skill in predicting futures in beef played him false. That guarantee of £7 per hundredweight turned out to be somewhat ahead of what Johnny Greene eventually obtained for his finished stock. Not, indeed, that my father derived any great pleasure from Johnny's miscalculation. Jack Keogh did not do *schadenfreude*. I doubt he even knew that German term for malicious enjoyment of another's misfortunes.

While the scheme of financing beef production was proving profitable, my father fretted about his risk exposure, mindful perhaps of his IMP experiences. Our 'Eureka moment' came about in a curious way. Out and about in Athboy one day I was approached by a dairy farmer who sought finance to expand his herd. Would the Livestock Credit Corporation advance him the money? Well, no, they would not. Dairy farmers kept their cows until they were only fit for the factory, if they had not already expired from old age. The dairy farmer persisted. How would it be if he signed an agreement with the creamery to which he supplied his milk whereby the Livestock Credit

Corporation would receive its monthly repayments before he received the balance?

How I avoided crashing in my haste to get back to our Dublin office I do not know. Within days we had canvassed the five principal Dublin dairies—Merville, Hughes Brothers, Lucan Dairies, Dublin Dairies and Tel-El-Kebir Dairies in Dun Laoghaire. In each instance it was merely a matter of pushing an open door. If their suppliers could increase their herds and thus their milk yields, each company's turnover could only increase, its profits correspondingly. It was, as they say, a 'win win' situation for all concerned.

As for the bankers, they were enchanted by the concept, embracing as it did guaranteed monthly repayments through suppliers of essential commodities. Particularly enthusiastic were those American banks that had set up Dublin branches in anticipation of agriculture-related business, forecast to explode when Ireland joined the Common Market. To their dismay they failed to make any inroads into a conservative market previously cornered by the two major Irish banks—Bank of Ireland and AIB, together with Ulster Bank. The Americans quietly folded their tents and withdrew, perplexed and disappointed.

By 1971 the Livestock Credit Corporation had facilities from eleven different banks, to the tune of £1.5m. Cows by then were fetching £300, whereby the LCC might be said to have owned, in varying degrees anyway, as many as 5,000 cows. From those original five Dublin dairies the LCC was by then dealing with fifty dairies, creameries and co-operatives countrywide. And all of this with just two sales reps on the road, dealing in every instance with the farmer in person, on his farm, assessing individual circumstances and the applicant's ability to meet his commitments.

In one respect the LCC had a remarkable record. Throughout the thirty years of its existence no customer ever claimed to have lost a single cow. On the face of it, this record is frankly incredible. God knows, many of 'our' cows must have died in debt. However, the potential loss of credit rating in the event of such a claim was in fact the LCC's guarantee against that eventuality. In any case, should one of 'our' cows died, the shortfall caused by her demise was simply spread across the remainder of the herd until the debt was redeemed.

The Livestock Credit Corporation folded its tent in 1988, after thirty successful years in business. The reason was simple. Over that period the number of active dairy farmers in Ireland shrank from 148,000 to less than 30,000. As the business became concentrated in larger and ever-larger holdings the smaller players sold their milk quotas and retired from that field of endeavour. The LCC had simply outlived its original function. Such is ever more the way of the commercial world. Fun while it lasted.

Actually, the life span of the Livestock Credit Corporation and the reasons for its eventual redundancy mirror the massive strides made in the dairy business in this country during that time. When the LCC came into being the national average milk yield per cow (during her eight-month lactation period) was 600 gallons. Today that figure stands at 900 gallons, with 2,000-gallon cows now quite commonplace.

A major breakthrough in this regard has to have been the introduction of artificial insemination (AI) in 1946. By 1972 it had become the normal practice, accounting for more than 60% of all cattle births. Moreover, the quality of the bulls utilized in this economical, efficient way was guaranteed superior to the aptly-named 'scrub bulls' or 'speakeasy bulls' to which impoverished farmers had all too often resorted. The composition of the national dairy herd simultaneously underwent a significant change. In 1960 James Dillon's favoured all-purpose shorthorns made up 80% of the dairy herd. By 1972 that proportion had shrunk to 40%, supplanted by Friesians, Hereford, Aberdeen Angus and those continental newcomers to which we will return.

Hand in hand with the upgrading of semen through AI and the alteration in breed types came a rapid growth of silage making as a substitute for traditional hay-making. Whereas hay is the hardest crop of all to save in our unpredictable, rainy climate, silage proves infinitely less problematic. Back in 1958, when the Livestock Credit Corporation was set up, just 2% of all Irish farmers made silage. By the end of the millennium that figure had risen to more than 55%. In that period Irish cattle farming had been transformed from cottage industry into agri-business.

Another measure of the tremendous structural changes in Irish agriculture during the lifetime of the Livestock Credit Corporation can be gleaned from Central Statistics Office figures. In 1960, two years after the LCC came into being, there were 92,400 farms of between 15 and 30 acres. By 1991, shortly after the LCC had run its course, that number of smallholdings had shrunk to 36,500. Over the same 30-year period farms of 100 acres or more had grown from 34,100 to 37,600.

As for dairy farmers, John Feehan gave their number in 1999 as 30,000, milking between them 1.5m cows. He predicted a decline in dairy farmers by 2016 to 20,000, which 'could well decline in time to half that number'.

Across the Irish Sea the story has been the same. How well I remember dairy farmer Paul Barber—a West Country man—after See More Business, owned in partnership with John Keightley, had won the 1999 Cheltenham Gold Cup. Paul told the press that he had two great ambitions in life: to milk 1,000 cows and to win the Gold Cup. Now he had realized both. Exactly ten years later Paul Barber faced the press again, having won his second Cheltenham

Gold Cup with Denman, owned in partnership with professional gambler Harry Findlay. This time Paul admitted to having revised those two ambitions in the interim. He had set his heart on winning a second Gold Cup, and milking 2,000 cows!

CHAPTER ELEVEN

Hunting Days

My father may have been no horseracing enthusiast, but he did approve of hunting. And so it was that I became a follower of the world famous Ward Union Staghounds—as my maternal grandfather Sheridan had been—shortly after my escape from Clongowes Wood College, having recovered from the scarlet fever to which I owed that happy release. By the time I hung up my boots in 2003 I had filled the posts of honorary secretary, master and chairman of the hunt.

Among the regular participants in my early days with the Ward Union I particularly remember Dr Bethel Solomons, obstetrician, gynaecologist and by that time President of the Royal College of Physicians in Ireland. Tall and distinguished, Bethel Solomons had played rugby for Ireland, capped ten times for his country. After one ignominious defeat the selectors had been castigated for fielding 'fourteen Protestants and a Jew'. It was a measure of the man that he delighted in recounting that story. Quite properly he insisted: 'while I am just as much an Irishman as I am a Jew, conversely, I am just as much a Jew as I am an Irishman.' As former Master of the Rotunda he warranted another reference explicit to all Dubliners. It had appeared in *Finnegan's Wake,* by Old Clongownian James Joyce: 'In the bethel of Solyman's I accouched their rotundities.'

For all that it has suffered as a political punchbag in recent times, the Ward Union has a distinguished history, its origins tracing back to two separate packs—the Dubber and the Hollywood—which hunted what is essentially the Ward Union country today. They became the Wards when amalgamated by a Mr Gerrard in 1830. From him the hounds passed to Captain John Stanley and thence to Peter Alley of New Park took them over in 1836.

Up to that time the Wards hunted 'bagged' foxes, until Peter Alley acquired some fallow deer, followed soon after by a number of red deer. In 1840 Lord Howth imported Mr Broadley's Staghounds from Leamington, keeping them with a subscription from the military until Lady Howth's death in 1842, whereupon Lord Howth sold the pack to the Dublin Garrison. In due course the Garrison Hounds, as they were called, became one with the Wards, around the time of the Crimean War (1854). That Crimean War accounted for at least one of the erstwhile masters, the Hon. 'Billy' Hutchinson, survived by his brother Lord Donoughmore and their cousin Richard Bernard. Their roll was filled by Charles and then Peter Alley until 1863, by which time he had recruited Charles Brindley as huntsman, ably assisted by his son Jem Brindley.

'Chorister' summarized the state of affairs during this period in this piece taken from 'Two Centuries of Fox-Hunting in Ireland', in *The Irish Horse*, 1957. 'Kilkenny was now the most important centre in the South East, Mallow on the South and Galway in the West, whilst from Dublin the rank and fashion of the day poured out into the plains of of Meath and Kildare to hunt stag with the Garrison pack, now the Ward Union, and fox with the County Hounds. In Meath, the Congill Hunt became the Meath Hunt in 1832, but it was not until 1851 that the famous Master, Mr Sam Reynell, developed the Dublin country as it is to-day.'

Writing in 1878 Bernard Fitzpatrick acknowledged the far-flung renown of the Ward Union in the days when the sun never set on the British Empire. 'The mention of the "Wards" recalls to the minds of many sportsmen, old and young, recollections of pleasant scenes, extraordinary feats, and happy hunting grounds. Their fame is more than European. In the new world as well as in the old they are spoken of with enthusiasm; and many there are whose destiny has placed them under the fierce glare of an Indian sun who owe some of their happiest hours to the "Wards".'

Hardly had those words appeared than the Ward Union welcomed its most celebrated visitor. On Monday, 24 February 1879, the members convened at Batterstown Halt

at 11.00 a.m., there to welcome a 'special' from Dublin carrying 40 other members and guests, together with their horses. The enlarged group then rode to nearby Parsonstown House, to await the arrival of their royal visitor, who had travelled by carriage the few miles from Summerhill House—the 'Irish Versailles'—rented as a hunting box from Hercules Rowley, Lord Langford. As ever, the Empress of Austria was to be piloted throughout the day by the dashing thruster 'Bay' Middleton. Their personal chemistry gave rise to speculation that would long outlive both of them.

The stag was enlarged and promptly led the pursuers south, past Moyglare, heading on by Maynooth to Maynooth College, where the team building a church in the grounds had breached the boundary wall to create a temporary gate. The stag dashed through, rescued by the builders from the chasing hounds. The temporary gate was closed. However, that aperture in the cut stone boundary wall, built to keep the seminarians in and worldly temptations out, proved no barrier to the leader of the hunt—Elizabeth, Empress of Austria, aboard Domino, a small bay hunter loaned her by Leonard Morrogh, became the first female ever to enter the hallowed precincts of Maynooth College.

The Queen of the Chase!
The Queen! Yes, The Empress!
Look, look how she flies,

With a hand that never fails
And a pluck that never dies.
The best man in England can't lead her—he's down!
'Bay' Middleton's back is done beautifully brown.
Hark horn and hark holloa!
Come on for a place!
He must ride who would follow
The Queen of the Chase!

Leonard Morrogh (1829-1889) was hailed as the Ward Union's greatest benefactor through his 'planting them in fee at Ashbourne'. That effectively meant that the upkeep of the Ward Union devolved upon a committee, as indeed it has remained ever since. In those more leisurely times the Wards hunted Monday, Wednesday and Saturday, using 32 couple of 'working hounds' for this purpose. In addition to fulfilling the honorary secretary's role for 25 years, Leonard Morrogh played a crucial part in the establishment of Fairyhouse racecourse and the Irish Grand National, first staged in 1870.

Political considerations ensured that Elizabeth of Austria—'Sisi' to her family—enjoyed just two seasons hunting in Ireland. As a token of her appreciation to Leonard Morrogh she had herself painted jumping a fence out hunting on Domino, by the Viennese equestrian artist Wilhelm Richter and duly sent the painting to him through the Ward Union committee. However, the committee decided the picture was intended not for one individual but for the hunt as a body. The committee prevailed and that painting still adorned the Ward Union committee room when John Welcome was researching his *The Sporting Empress—The Story of Elizabeth of Austria and Bay Middleton* in the 1970s. Having resigned the field mastership of the Ward Union in 1883, Leonard Morrogh retired to live in Wexford, where he was killed in a fall out hunting with his local pack in January 1889. In the same month Crown Prince Rudolph, Sisi's troubled son, shot his female companion and then himself in a hunting lodge at Mayerling.

Sisi lived to learn of Bay Middleton's death while riding in a race at Kineton in 1892, having previously declared that it was to be his last time to don colours, aged forty-six. By then Sisi had long ceased hunting, wandering instead round Europe and the Mediterranean. In 1898 her travels had taken her to Geneva, where she was fatally stabbed by a French-Italian anarchist, Luigi Lucheni.

The iconic status that Elizabeth of Austria had long since attained in Ward Union lore was refreshed in October 2010 when a hunting whip that she had carried and subsequently presented to Captain Robert Fowler, Master of the Meath Foxhounds in 1879 came up for auction in Slane Castle. Decorated with a silver band bearing the Hapsburg imperial crest, it had been discovered in Rahinstown, the

Fowlers' ancestral home and valued by James Adam and Son anywhere between €3,000 and €5,000. It attracted enquiries from both the Austrian Embassy and the Schönbrunn Palace in Vienna. An anonymous collector in the Channel Islands had the final say at €37,000.

Another name writ large in the annals of the Ward Union Hunt is Percy Maynard, the most popular and respected field master in the hunt's history prior to becoming master himself. Traditionally the mastership brought with it an invitation to become a steward at the annual Ward Union Hunt Steeplechases, as Fairyhouse's annual Easter Monday fixture was long known. The locals tended to refer to it as 'the Dubs' day out'. Percy's death just prior to the 1918 renewal led to a race there being named in his honour—the Percy Maynard Memorial.

When I made my début with the Ward Union in 1948 the joint masters were Andrew Levins Moore and George Malcomson, the latter sharing the secretarial duties with Stanislaus Lynch. Besides being good men across that formidable country bisected by the Ashbourne Road, both men had demonstrated their prowess in colours, both on the racecourse proper and 'between the flags'. Andrew Moore had succeeded Judge Wylie as master. Eric Craigie described his reign thus in his delightful memoirs, *An Irish Sporting Life*. 'Andrew Moore became master in 1939 and I consider him the best Master the

Ward ever had or will have. Hunting during his term of office was amazingly good; he was a fearless rider, knew his country and left the hunting of the hounds to his huntsman, Tom Fitzsimons. Andrew was most popular with the farmers and was a keen competitor at point-to-points.' As for Stanislaus, he was every bit as adept with the pen as he was skilled in the saddle. Should you fancy the sensation of riding in an Irish Grand National from the safety of your armchair, I strongly recommend Stanislaus's 'Over the fences at Fairyhouse' to be found in his *Echoes of the Hunting Horn*.

It became my turn to act as honorary secretary in 1961, relieving Donald Craigie and Eric Craigie, who had become joint master with the long-serving George Malcomson from 1959. Standish Collen then relieved George, as joint master with Eric until 1967. Eric Craigie described why he stopped with brutal candour. 'My last hunt was from Garristown in 1967. I lost my nerve. I pulled off early and resigned as master that season. Never to back a horse again. It's something I didn't think would happen.' Frank Roe and I took up the baton. Twenty enjoyable seasons shared with such as Tom Mangan, Roy Craigie and Denis Coakley saw me step aside in 1986, then to become chairman.

Down the years I was often asked to compare stag hunting with foxhunting, to my embarrassment, for I had little experience of the latter. But there was one consolation. My questioner had to have been equally naïve about stag hunting to ask in the first place. The greatest difference is in the time each pursuit takes. With the staghounds a good run should ideally last about an hour and a half, lickety spit from flagfall. Three hours would be an exceptional chase. Recapture at the end of the run required the intervention of three or more hardy farmers to bundle the exhausted quarry into its trailer safe from the panting hounds. By contrast, a dogged master of foxhounds could keep the field out until nightfall, determined to bolt and hunt a fox to the kill.

We hunted both stags and hinds, typically three times in any season. In this we relied totally on our dedicated huntsman Eamon Dunphy, who was responsible for the care and conditioning of the deer, which were kept in a 15-acre park. We used to import them from Captain Lucas in Surrey, in addition to breeding some of our own. Deer lose a lot of weight in the course of a hunt and so they need to carry plenty of condition before being loosed to give their pursuers the thrills and spills of the chase. Moreover, as fast and agile as they are, deer need a decent start to avoid becoming stags at bay too soon. To this end we relied on Eamon to recruit larger, slower cast-offs from foxhound packs, from which he selected the best to develop our own breed of slow but resolute staghounds.

Invariably things did not always go to plan, particularly when the quarry for the day was a big, bullish stag that would sometimes refuse to run, standing his ground and bellowing defiance at his expectant pursuers. Ere too long that burly boyo was 'added to the list', in genteel, if dated racing parlance. He became a 'havier'. Not a word you will find in any normal dictionary, it means a gelded stag.

As the only surviving staghound pack in the 26 counties—outlasting the Roscommon and Templemore packs—the Ward Union has an undeserved reputation for posing more risk to horse and rider than to those who pursue the fox or the hare on horseback. I suppose one could say that staghunting is akin to an old-fashioned point-to-point (called redcoat races). Unlike foxhunting it offers few checks, rare pauses. Yet its very brevity ensures the horses do not get unduly fatigued, for most falls are incurred on tiring horses that begin to take chances with fences. As a matter of fact, the only human fatality I can recall in all my years out with the Wards was poor Major Tony Burke of Stackallan Stud, killed when his horse suffered a heart attack.

Stanislaus Lynch described the Ward country to a nicety in *A Huntsman's Paradise*. 'The Ward Union country is noted for its wide and sometimes very deep ditches. Although the Ward hounds pursue their stag almost at steeplechase pace, a clever horse who knows the country will slow down at each fence and will make up for lost time by galloping fast in the great big stretches of grassland between his fences. The reason he slows is because a Ward ditch is usually too wide to take at racing pace. His proper technique is to crawl down portion of the way on the take-off side of the fence, then make a cat-like spring across the ditch to the opposite slope, where a short upwards jerk will bring him back up to ground level and into the next field. This applies even should a hedge be growing on one or both sides of an open ditch.

'While the description of these fences may tend unavoidably to make them appear more difficult than they are, the visitor can rest assured that the negotiation of them can, with almost perfect safety, be left entirely to the experienced judgement of an honest Irish hunting horse.'

Looking back on my days with the Wards, one of my most pleasurable recollections concerns our cordial relationship with the farmers who made us welcome across their lands. While tact and diplomacy were often required, it surely helped that Denis Coakley supplied the feed for their cattle, the Craigies took their milk into Merville (later Premier) Dairies and the Livestock Credit Corporation offered financing when that was not otherwise easy to obtain. Does the current buzz word 'Troika' describe the situation?

CHAPTER TWELVE

Land Commission

To many like my father, who had invested his wartime 'touch' with that Waterford abattoir to become the owner of 500 acres of prime pasture land, the elephant in the Irish agricultural kitchen was that fearsome, all-powerful institution—the Land Commission. As a prelude to revealing the Keogh family's experiences with that institution, it is important to comprehend the political background and consequences of the Land Commission.

The Irish Land Commission was created in 1881 as a rent fixing commission by the Land Law (Ireland) Act 1881, also known as the second Irish Land Act. For a century it was the body responsible for re-distributing farmland in Ireland.

With the Ashbourne Act 1885 the Commission developed into a tenant-purchasing commission and assisted in the agreed transfer of freehold farmland from landlord to tenant. This was a response to the turbulent land war that had started in 1879. It was rapidly enacted by the government of Lord Salisbury, funded originally with £5,000,000 and was designed to avert support for the Irish Parliamentary

Party, given the larger number of voters allowed by the Reform Act 1884, before the IPP entered its alliance with William Ewart Gladstone in 1886.

The Commission eventually transferred 13.5 million acres (55,000 sq. km.) by 1920. Following the Land Conference of December 1902 arranged by George Wyndham (a conservative minister and Chief Secretary for Ireland, but also descended from Lord Edward FitzGerald), the revolutionary Wyndham Land (Purchase) Act 1903 was orchestrated through parliament by William O'Brien MP, which provided government finance to buy out freeholds, with the former tenant farmers paying back the capital over 68 years. This was managed by the Land Commission, along with such ancillary work as compiling statistics. Valuations were reckoned on a 'years purchase' (Y.P.) basis, the price being a multiple (18-24 times) the annual rent. The Commission had to supervise the haggling process and find the fairest multiple for every transfer. The loans issued by the government were resold in the capital markets as 'Land Bonds'.

History may have demonized the Land Commission for its role in land redistribution, but the truth is rather different. Many landlords, by then heavily in debt, were only too ready to sell up, provided the receipts could be used to discharge their liabilities. In 1903 the Duke of Leinster sold 41,000 acres for £786,000. The King-Harmans realized

£625,000 for 70,000 acres of less productive land. Their 'success' encouraged others to replace rental income with investment, notably Lord Fitzwilliam (53,000 acres) and Lord Longford (9,000 acres). As for the Liberal peer Lord Dunraven: 'this generous settlement which at one leap solved age-old contentious ownership of Irish land was only to be welcomed . . . a lasting monument to what the spirit can accomplish for Ireland. It changed the face of the country; improvement was almost miraculous. In five years it enabled 228,938 occupying tenants to buy their holding.'

Melanie Hall, ever-helpful custodian of the Land Commission archive in Portlaoise, drew an intriguing comparison between the Land Commission of its time and our present-day National Asset Management Agency (NAMA). Melanie made the valid point that the opportunity to sell up for guaranteed payment came as a Godsend to many impoverished landlords. In fact so many availed of this scheme that the Land Commission soon became a virtual land bank of Ireland. As such the Land Commission reserved the right to repossess farms that it considered were not being utilized in the manner intended, principally by recipients who elected to live and work elsewhere than on the lands provided, in some instances even sub-letting their holding.

By 1908 the emerging problem was whether the new owners would be economically viable on their small farms.

Michael McDonnell commented that: 'The breaking up of the grazing lands, which in many instances the landlords are keeping back from the market, has not met with much success under the Act, and it is difficult to see how compulsion is to be avoided if the country is to be saved from the economically disastrous position of having established in it a number of occupying owners on tenancies which are not large enough to secure to them a living wage.'

It was realized by now that existing rural poverty arose from small farm sizes, yet the Act's procedures and limits also tended to keep farm sizes down. The aim had been to create 'peasant proprietors' owning what were usually small farms. By definition the activists in the 1880s Land War period had been poorer and more desperate, and few came from larger prosperous farms. This remained a matter of policy debate for the rest of the Commission's existence; generally it continued to create new small units by breaking up larger units that had more commercial potential. Larger commercial farmers were characterized as 'landlords' or 'grazers' simply because they had more land than average.

A further Land Act in 1909 fostered by the liberal Chief Secretary for Ireland Augustine Birrell allowed for land to be bought by the Commission by compulsory purchase. In 1915 Birrell confirmed in parliament that all Irish land transfers from 1884 to the end of 1914 had cost the British government £91,768,450, and the tenants had invested a further £1,584,516. By then the stream of landlords willing to sell had become a torrent, stemmed only be the government's inability to fund the mutually desired transfers. Lord Clonbrock, with 28,246 acres in east Galway, had set his face against selling any of his holding in 1903. By 1915 increased agitation and falling incomes led him to sell almost all his estate.

On the formation of the Irish Free State in 1922 the Commission was reconstituted by the Land Law (Commission) Act, 1923, which also dissolved the Congested Districts Board. Provision was made for compulsory purchase of land owned by a non-Irish citizen. Untenanted land could now be compulsorily purchased and divided out to local families; this was applied unevenly across the country, with some large estates surviving if the owners could show that their land was being actively farmed. Many who had formerly described themselves as 'landlords' now called themselves 'farmers' as indeed they were, whether farming untenanted acres in their own right, or renting to 'grazers' on the conacre system. It proved much easier to collect monies due from grazers than it had ever been from dozens of small, impoverished tenant farmers, with consequent savings on such as quit rents, head rents, improvements and bailiffs' salaries,

The extent to which the old landowning structure remained nevertheless intact was reflected in such remaining holdings as the Marquess of Lansdowne (49,000 acres in Kerry), the Earl of Leitrim (39,000 acres in Donegal), Lord Farnham (20,000 acres in Cavan), Lady Edith Wyndham (11,000 acres in Monaghan) and the Kavanaghs with 7,000 acres in Carlow. Against that, the Congested Districts Board, between its inception in 1891 and its dissolution in 1923, had purchased 874 estates totalling 1.77 million acres for £8.9 million, primarily along the western seaboard.

From 1923 the amounts outstanding were paid to the British government as 'land annuities', accruing in a Land Purchase Fund. This was fixed at £250,000 annually in 1925. In December 1925 William Cosgrave lamented that there were already '250,000 owners of uneconomic holdings, the holdings of such a valuation as did not permit of a decent livelihood for the owners'. Despite this, his government continued to subdivide larger landholdings, primarily to solicit electoral support. While that may be true, it must be said that the worldwide economic depression had ruined many of the remaining landowners, who had seen both their investment and agricultural incomes all but wiped out. At a time when land had become virtually worthless, through a combination of land-grabbing and general agitation, the Land Commission provided a lifeline in many cases.

Under the powers of compulsory acquisition granted to the Land Commission in 1926 alone Lord Leitrim was deprived of 20,300 acres, Lord Farnham of 11,300, Lord Ashtown of 9,000, Viscount de Vesci of 10,000 and Lord Powerscourt of 6,800, each of them compensated in 4.5% per annum land bonds.

The Land Act of 1933, passed on a vote of 70-39, allowed the Minister for Finance to divert the annuities for local government projects. This was the factor that caused the 'Economic War' in 1933-38, and was mutually resolved by a one-off payment of £10m to Britain in 1938. From 1932 the government argued strongly that Irish farmers should no longer be obliged for historic reasons to pay Britain for Irish land, but when Britain had passed out of the payment system it illogically still required farmers to continue to pay their annuities to it as before. In the Dáil Frank Aiken famously declared 'the day of the lazy rancher is over'. In fact, the actions of his party ensured that industrious and lazy alike faced ruin; the average price of cattle exported declining from £16 to £8 from 1931 to 1935, with total values plummeting from £12.7m to £4.3m.

In 1983 the Commission ceased acquiring land; this signified the start of the end of the Commission's reform of Irish land ownership, though freehold transfers of farmland still had to be signed off by the Commission into the 1990s. The Commission was dissolved on 31 March 1999 by the Irish Land Commission (Dissolution) Act, 1992 and most of the remaining liabilities and assets

At Christina's wedding, October 1962 (L TO R) Adam Mullan, Jack Carlin,
Joan Keogh and Tony Bruton

Uncle Christopher, an enthusiastic and
accomplished amateur artist

Pamela Magnier with
ex-master Raymond Keogh

Sean Byrne, master, with Raymond Keogh and Joe Hardy

Miriam and Susan Craigie at the opening meet, Ashbourne, 1967

Frank Roe, joint-master of the Ward Union, with Mrs Brophy at the 1967 Naas Harriers Hunt Ball

Fellow cattleman Jimmy O'Connell with Mr Smarty, the horse he owned and trained to win the 1967 Irish Cesarewitch

Denis Coakley, joint-master, making the presentation to Mrs Gloria O'Donoghue at the Ward Union point-to-point meeting

Trainer Stuart Murless with Sea Break

Nocturnal Spree winning the 1975 One Thousand Guineas by a short head

*Anne O'Kelly leading Nocturnal Spree into
the Newmarket winner's enclosure*

Irian (Anne Ferris), bought on a whim

Irian (right) fighting it out with Twinburn over the last.
At the line Irian and Ann Ferris prevailed by a short head

L to R Michael, Johnny, Helene and Gene Kruger

Ken O'Reilly Hyland, Gene Kruger, Johnny Henry and Michael

My fabulous five and me

were transferred to the Minister for Agriculture and Food. Many relevant historical records are held by the National Archives of Ireland.

The Commission, whilst often regarded as the champion of land ownership for those who used it, and social justice, was not without controversy. In particular its subdivision of land into uneconomic units has had a lasting effect, as well as the destruction of fine landlords' residences such as Monellan Castle and Shanbally Castle with Government approval.

Monellan Castle—otherwise the 'Big House' dominating the Finn Valley in Donegal—was built in the 1700s for the Delap family, remaining in their ownership until the 1930s. The Reverend Robert Delap built St Anne's Church of Ireland, becoming its first minister. He was buried standing up in the grounds of St Anne's. His headstone had to be repaired several times as his coffin gradually rotted away. Robert's daughter occupied Monellan Castle until it was acquired by the Land Commission. On the orders of the government of the day Monellan Castle was demolished in the 1930s, the stone used to build better houses for some of the small farmers in the vicinity and also in road building. The remaining demesne wall, three miles long, contains forestry under the management of Coillte.

Two decades later Shanbally Castle, Clogheen, Tipperary, suffered a similar fate, as Randall McDonnell recorded in *The Lost Houses of Ireland*. 'Of all the 'lost' houses in this collection, Shanbally Castle is the most tragic. Not only was the building of the first importance in the history of Irish domestic architecture but it was also in good and complete condition before it fell foul of the crass ignorance and prejudice of the bureaucrats who decided to destroy it. It was the largest castle that John Nash ever built in Ireland—Nash was the Prince Regent's architect, and his white terraces and wide thoroughfares, such as Regent Street, may still be seen in London. Nash's other castles in Ireland were Ravensworth, Caerhays and Aqualate. Shanbally also had the distinction that it was built, not for the descendant of some Cromwellian carpetbagger, but for the scion of an old Irish family: Cornelius O'Callaghan.'

As farming became more mechanized from the 1930s foreign investment in commercial farms was discouraged, reducing overall farm output. Often the buyers found it hard to earn enough to live a good life, as found in the poems of Patrick Kavanagh. The Dáil report from the 1920s to the 1960s frequently include questions about the division of former estates, and the acquisition of land with public finance on favourable terms for constituents via the Land Commission was understood as a way for politicians to gain electoral support.

From 1940 a minority in Fianna Fáil and Coalition cabinets consistently argued for larger farms to be encouraged, instead of sponsoring new small farmers that often had too little capital, skills or enthusiasm. This was successfully opposed for electoral reasons by de Valera, and in Coalition governments by Joseph Blowick, the leader of Clann na Talmhan.

Under the 1923 Act busier farmers had to rent land under an 11-month or seasonal 'conacre' system, as longer arrangements could cause an owner to lose his farm by compulsory purchase by the Land Commission. While there were now over 200,000 Irish landowners compared to a tiny fraction of that number in the 1800s, the basic term for the use of the land had reverted back to the norm of the 1860s, with no rights to renew a lease and no incentive to improve rented land. By 1980 some 860,000 acres (3,500 sq. km.) were rented annually under conacre, suggesting a new imbalance between mere ownership and the more active farmers.

Just how deeply emotive the issue of land ownership remained in the Irish psyche long after independence became apparent in the 1950s when W.H. Harold, a Norfolk farmer and his partners invested £70,000 to purchase two estates of prime agricultural land in Carlow. In 1951 they bought Browne's Hill, adding Oak Park in 1957, 2,100 acres in total. The sheer size of either estate had put it beyond the reach of local farmer. As such the syndicate was able to purchase both for the bargain price of £34 per acre, less than half the average £80 per acre current for smaller holdings and closer to to the annual rate for conacre.

W.H. Harold continued to brave local hostility, visiting the properties each month, until he received an envelope bearing an Irish postmark and containing a single bullet. That marked the outset of what became known as the 'Carlow Land War'. Its leader was Kathleen Brady of Bennekerry, daughter of a neighbouring small farmer and a founder member of the local land club. Brendan Behan dubbed her the Joan of Arc of small farmers, while the radical Peadar O'Donnell cleverly advised former Government Minister Gerry Boland that Harold's life was at risk. His advice bore fruit. When W.H. Harold next arrived in Dublin airport he was met by a Garda escort for his trip down to Carlow. It was his last such visit. Within a month W.H. Harold informed the Land Commission of his willingness to dispose of both properties. The Land Commission purchased Oak Park for £68,000 (Harold had given £55,000 for it three years earlier). Seven hundred acres were allocated to local farmers, while the Agricultural Institute took over the big house and remaining land as a research centre.

Meanwhile the Carlow land club continued its protests. One such, on Friday, 8 August 1958, attracted 30 land clubs and several thousand farmers from all over the country. Such was the media interest BBC television sent over a documentary crew to cover the event, the programme subsequently broadcast in Britain, America and Canada.

During this period Ireland contained 135,000 family farms of 30 acres or less. The protests were directed not just at foreign buyers, but equally at the Land Commission and the Government for their inaction. The latter was taunted by banners reminding it of earlier electoral pledges: 'The land of Ireland for the people of Ireland.'

The consequent Lands Act 1965 was passed to restrict new foreign investment in agriculture, some of which was speculatively based upon Ireland's imminent entry to the European Economic Community that eventually occurred in 1973. The EEC's 'Four Freedoms' allowed for unlimited investment anywhere in the EEC by any citizen of any EEC member state. This naturally undermined the ethos of the Land Commission, which had purchased a further 807,000 acres (3,270 sq. km.) since 1923. By the early 1970s half of open land purchases were by non-farmers, and half of those were buy small sites, typically for building bungalows.

Geographer Frank Mitchell provided this overview, penned in 1976. 'In Ireland in 1900 everyone was rejoicing that the tyranny of large estates was over, and that the land now belonged to the small farmers of Ireland. But less than a hundred years later the horrid thought is beginning to arise that there was something to be said for large estates.'

By the 1980s, just before its reform, the Land Commission came under the Department of Lands, which was in turn a part of the Department of Agriculture. The Department of Lands was seen as an overgrown entity, employing 750 people in 1983; its budget of IR£15m included IR£8m for administration costs and only IR£7m for actual land purchase or division. Further purchases were suspended that year by Paul Connaughton.

So much for the general; time to become more specific. Land hunger throughout Ireland continued unabated into the latter half of the twentieth century. Under constant pressure to 'stripe' large landholdings and redistribute them as smaller, uneconomical parcels, the Land Commission cast its beady eye on our 250-acre holding in Roestown. It issued proceedings for what it termed 'resumption'.

Roestown had been acquired by the Land Commission from the estate of one Captain Edward George Woods. It had then been leased to the family of John D. Kennedy, who emigrated to the United States, unfortunately at the time of the Depression. The Land Commission had begun measures to 'resume' these lands from the Kennedys as early as 1930. Six years later the bulky files reveal that the Kennedys were prepared to surrender, subject to a decent offer, which was not forthcoming.

When John D. Kennedy returned to Ireland at the outbreak of the Second World War, the Land Commission made another attempt to 'resume' Roestown. Kennedy had protested successfully that he intended to marry and build a house on the land. Some time later John Kennedy changed his mind, enquiring whether anyone would take the property off his hands. He was directed to my father, who was then flush and in the market. The price asked was £3,500. My father agreed to buy Kennedy's tenancy, but deducted £500 on the basis that the Land Commission might renew its longstanding campaign at any time . . .

Exactly ten years later the Land Commission made another move to 'resume' Roestown. An order for compulsory purchase followed swiftly. In cases where the landowners claimed essential necessity for retention of their lands, their recourse was to the Land's own court of appeal— Cúirt Choimisiún Talún na h-Éireann. It sat opposite Government Buildings, now the site of the Merrion Hotel.

To my father the Roestown farm represented the bulk of his security for himself and his family. However, that in itself did not justify grounds for retention in the political climate which then prevailed. He and I needed to evolve a more complex, more imaginative line of defence. We pleaded that our lands were vital to the successful continuation of our business—the acquisition, finishing and then export of cattle, vital to the country's economy, to its crucial balance of payments. We likened it to a manufacturing premises. Furthermore, it was not an overnight development. The Keoghs had depended upon similar landholdings to serve the national interest throughout four generations. It worked.

CHAPTER THIRTEEN

Enter the Charolais

Looking back over my lifetime in the cattle trade the single most momentous development for me was the introduction of Charolais cattle in 1964. It effectively transformed the Irish national herd. Far from happening overnight—as many innovations tend to do—this watershed in the Irish cattle trade only came to pass after a long, tortuous campaign, initiated by an Englishman.

Laurie Gardner, the instigator of this ground-breaking project, died as long ago as 1969. Fortunately, his son Shan, a successful auctioneer in Victoria, New South Wales, has kindly weighed in with recollections of his father, a major in the 8th Airborne during the Second World War. Let him tell the story in his own way.

'After the war, you can imagine how these men coped, some well, some not so well. They never spoke about their experiences. Now, how my father came to the West of Ireland I was never told. All I can do is put down on paper some of the knowledge that I have. Dad was offered the Seat of Windsor and Slough for the Conservative Party and declined, the remuneration being too paltry.

'My father was very well travelled, highly intelligent, a fighter, a thinker who was never endowed with money.

His father—my grandfather—Sir Ernest Gardner was MP for Windsor and Slough for 13 years. Knighted in the reign of Queen Victoria, under the Prime Ministership of Benjamin Disraeli, my grandfather died aged 69 when my father was nine. My father was the youngest, along with three sisters. One of his sisters, Dame Violet Quist, was the leading lady heart specialist in Harley Street.

'His friends in life were across the spectrum—West of Ireland pubs a favourite. If you Google Sir John Hackett (Shan Hackett, my godfather)—they were great friends— you will get an idea of what my father got up to in his youth after he left Bradfield College.

'Dad and Lord Louis Mountbatten married sisters and were the best of friends; Lord Louis in Sligo, Dad in Enniscrone, Couty Sligo and Ballina, County Mayo. He had a successful chicken hatchery business in Ballina— 'Ideal Chicks'—sold to Thornbers. Day-old chicks were exported to the UK and Europe regularly.

'He researched whatever he was interested in very thoroughly . . . did not suffer fools gladly . . . a fair and generous man, highly thought of by his peers.'

Whereas Shan has no memory of how or why his father made his way to Ireland after the war, setting up his business in Ballina and selling it on for substantial profit, former Irish champion jockey Willie Robinson has kindly provided that key. Laurie Gardner, a lifelong racing man, had served in the war with Major Cyril Hall. The latter had been appointed as the first manager of the Irish National Stud when it was set up in 1946. Cyril Hall advised his fellow-officer that government grants for setting up businesses in Ireland were generous; increasingly generous the further west one went. Hence Ballina.

As stable jockey to Dan Moore in the late 'Fifties and early 'Sixties, Willie Robinson rode Commutering to win the 1960 Galway Hurdle and the 1961 Powers Gold Cup in Laurie Gardner's 'Black, pink sleeves & cap'. Moreover, Willie married Susan Hall, Cyril's daughter. Always regarded as a 'lucky' owner, Laurie Gardner also had a succession of flat horses with Curragh trainer Dick McCormick, winning the 1959 Phoenix Park '1500' with Gigi. Never afraid to spend money when in funds, Laurie Gardner was reputed to have given £25,000 for Die Hard at the close of the 1960 flat season. He recouped a fair portion when Vincent O'Brien sent out Die Hard to win the 1961 Ebor Handicap at York under Lester Piggott.

The health of the Gardner bank balance was naturally not unaffected by his three marriages. Shan, his son, has this to say about Laurie's first 'marriage'. 'Mary (née Cassel) was first married to Cunningham-Reid, a well known fish restaurateur in London. Noel, her eldest son, won Le Mans alongside Tony Brooks. Her youngest was in jail in the Rift Valley (for shooting the natives).

'Her second marriage was to my father . . . They were on honeymoon in Bali at the outbreak of World War II. Dad flew home, she returned by sea. End of marriage. . . Her third marriage was to Lord Delamere—for a short time.'

Laurie Gardner subsequently married Erica de Rougement, a Swiss-German and mother of their two sons Shan and Nick. Laurie's third and final wife was another Swiss, Elizabeth 'Liz' Mulheim.

As to how Laurie Gardner made the quantum leap from day-old chickens to Charolais cattle, let Shan reiterate his father's thinking at that time. 'It was well known that the breeders were breeding cattle that were 'too pretty' in the British Isles. Something had to be done to breed more scope, more size, less fat into them. What's more, marbling in European breeds was a decisive 'plus'. With this in mind the exercise was begun . . .'

Paddy O'Keeffe, founding editor of the *Irish Farmers Journal*, recalls the story as though it were yesterday. It seems that during his wartime service in France Laurie Gardner's enquiring mind had noted the large white cattle unlike any he had ever seen in Britain. First recorded in France as long ago as 878, Charolais cattle had been selectively bred over the ensuing millennium as large, docile sources of milk, beef and haulage. However, it was not until they were displaced in the last-named function by the introduction of tractors and lorries after the First

World War that the single Charolais herd book came into being. The breed standard was then modified to emphasize physical conformation and thickness of muscular tissues, thereby achieving large carcase weights with maximum meat content, minimum fat and other waste material.

For all its obvious virtues, this breed centred round the northwestern districts of Niverne and Saone-sur-Loire only began to attract the attention of overseas producers in the 1950s. Brazil started the trend in 1950, followed by Argentina and South Africa in 1955. Breeders in those countries sought to maximize the value of bull calves born to their dairy herds, as traditionally male offspring of milch cows commanded low prices owing to their paltry beef content. By 1964 French exports of Charolais stood at 259 bulls and 1,605 cows.

The Irish economy was still very heavily dependent on beef exports in the 1960s. Indeed, the countrywide railway system survived primarily to transport cattle from all over Ireland—directly or indirectly—to the Dublin cattle market and thence to Britain, on the hoof. However, deep-seated fear of contagious epidemics—notably foot and mouth—saw the official mindset adamantly opposed to the introduction of any new breeds from countries where such epidemics remained commonplace. Memories of the 1942 outbreak of foot and mouth remained still too fresh in too many minds. Well used to dealing with the Department of Agriculture in his editorial capacity, Paddy O'Keeffe had become familiar with the innate conservatism and resistance to change in bureaucratic circles.

Laurie Gardner's realization of the necessity to begin political lobbying led him to the editor of the *Irish Farmers Journal*. Well connected at all levels of the Irish agricultural scene by virtue of his position, Paddy O'Keeffe must have entrée to those who could bring the appropriate influence to bear on an ultra-conservative Department of Agriculture. Not surprisingly, Paddy knew them all, from Taoiseach Seán Lemass down. But when Paddy grasped Laurie Gardner's ground-breaking objective it occurred to him that it was not Seán Lemass but his ambitious son-in-law, Charles J. Haughey, who might constitute the most effective agent of change. To this end Paddy reminded Laurie Gardner that there was no such thing as a free lunch, which the latter well knew. He was playing for high stakes. The chips were likely to prove expensive.

Not content to rely entirely on political influence, Laurie also used Paddy O'Keeffe's contacts to canvass the leading players in the beef trade, among them my father and Frank Quinn. Laurie reasoned that if he could convince the meat processors of the added benefits of the larger, leaner Charolais cattle—particularly for the European export market—he would recruit more widespread support for his campaign. Actually, Laurie Gardner's methodical approach and strategical procedure quickly persuaded Paddy that the former's wartime activities must have encompassed rather more that straightforward military combat. As Shan has observed, Laurie and his fellow-combatants never spoke of their wartime experiences, unless, perhaps, among one another.

Born in 1925 and a partner in the Dublin accountancy firm of Haughey Boland, Charles J. Haughey married Maureen Lemass in 1951, entering the Dáil as an elected TD in 1957. Promotion had been swift. Appointed parliamentary secretary to the Minister for Justice within two years, he became Minister for Justice in 1961, holding that office until 1964, when he assumed the Agriculture portfolio. It was as Minister for Justice that Charles J. Haughey joined the ranks of racehorse owners, registering his 'Black, blue sash & cap' in 1962. Nor did he have long to wait before tasting racecourse. Dick McCormick saddled Miss Cossie to win for her new owner at Navan in July 1962. Dick had earlier done likewise for Miss Cossie's previous owner—Laurie Gardner.

Paddy O'Keeffe vividly recalled the initial meeting between Laurie Gardner and Charles J. Haughey, over lunch in the Red Bank, of happy memory. When the former excused himself towards the end of the meal the Minister confided to Paddy that his father-in-law was keen to see his son-in-law acquire a residence more befitting his position. He had his eye on just such a house, asking price £10,000. Would yer man be good for the necessary loan? Intrigued that the Minister should come to the point so quickly, Paddy suggested there was nothing to be lost by asking. Laurie Gardner never even blinked, pulling out his cheque book and filling out a cheque for the amount in question.

In due course that momentous encounter between the Minister and the aspiring cattle importer bore fruit. In response to the Department of Agriculture's flat refusal to entertain the importation of cattle from the continent, the resourceful Minister had overcome the Department's stringent quarantine stipulations in a most creative fashion. He had commandeered Spike Island for that very purpose. While Spike Island was to prove the ultimate location, the equally resourceful Laurie Gardner had earlier leased East Calf Island off Baltimore in west Cork, constructing a landing slip whereby the cattle could be landed safely.

Spike Island, in the Lee estuary below Cork, had been a British military garrison since acquired in 1779 when Fort Westmoreland had been built there to guard against the threat of French attack on the important trading port of Cork. Later a prison and convict depot, housing such as John Mitchell, prior to transportation to Botany Bay and other penal settlements, Spike Island had gained the reputation of 'Ireland's Alcatraz'. It had been adapted as an internment camp for IRA suspects in 1921, am(

those incarcerated there being Michael Collins's brother. As late as 1924 it had featured in an ambush of British soldiers and civilians, machine-gunned on a launch returning from that outpost by men in Free State army uniform. The Free State Government had immediately issued a disclaimer, condemning this atrocity calculated to destabilize the fledgling state. As part of one of the Treaty Ports, Spike Island was only handed over to the Irish Government in 1938. Later still 'Spike Island' remained a constant threat to any seen to pose a threat to the stability of the de Valera Government.

In that capacity Spike Island continued in use as both a military base for both the regular Irish Army and the FCA and as a prison. As it was no longer utilized in either capacity by 1964, Spike Island was an ideal location as a quarantine station for the Charolais cattle that were believed to hold the key to transforming Ireland's beef herd. In 1964 the Department of Agriculture purchased and installed an initial draft of 8 bulls and 10 heifers. Once proven disease-free, these were followed by a second consignment of 4 bulls and 42 heifers, the majority acquired by a select group of private cattle breeders, destined to reap a handsome return on their outlay. This elite comprised Raymond Guest, US Ambassador to Ireland, stud owner Alan Lillingston, business mogul Paddy McGrath and John Mooney, founder of the *Irish Farmers Journal*.

To ensure the success of this ground-breaking venture Paddy O'Keeffe had sought the advice of the leading French cattle geneticists. That contact led to a flying visit to France, the entourage comprising the Minister for Agriculture, Laurie Gardner, Paddy O'Keeffe and Frank Quinn of Irish Meat Packers (IMP). The brief visit concluded with a dinner in Paris. The Minister for Agriculture sought Laurie's advice on the question of bringing a female companion to the event, accustomed as he had become to seeking Laurie's advice on many matters of protocol and etiquette. Laurie gave his distinctly guarded consent and the evening passed off successfully. However, when the Minister for Agriculture came down to breakfast the following morning, accompanied by said female companion, Laurie Gardner's patience snapped, as he made clear in the plainest terms. Lady friends—and Laurie was actually more explicit— might perhaps have their place of an evening, but he was damned if they were welcome at breakfast!

Sadly, the pioneer of this revolution in Irish cattle breeding was not destined to relish his success for long. Ill-health and the necessity for a warmer climate prompted Laurie to invest in a coffee plantation in Kenya, returning to Ireland for occasional visits. Paddy O'Keeffe recalled Laurie's final visit, entertaining Laurie and Liz to lunch *en route* to their stay with Peter Patrick and Anne Hemphill in Tulira Castle. Laurie Gardner, 55 and already severely incapacitated by multiple sclerosis, died when his car, in which he was a passenger, left the road between Loughrea and Ballinasloe in June 1969.

Half a century after Ireland opened her doors to the Charolais, continental breeds have proliferated here, notably Simmental, Limousin, Blonde d'Aquitaine, Aubrac, Saler and Belgian Blue. That meeting brokered by Paddy O'Keeffe between Charles J. Haughey and Laurie Gardner had indeed altered the nature of the Irish beef herd, in perpetuity.

CHAPTER FOURTEEN

Marriage and Family

Thank goodness for proof readers, a species of which I was blissfully ignorant until well into this memoir, as I have been taught to call it. One such quizzical proof reader invited me to confirm that I had gone through life without ever acquiring a wife or having a family. True enough, in my obsession with the cattle business and the changes I had lived through in that regard my family had somehow been completely overlooked. *Mea culpa*!

Improbable as this must sound, comfortably ensconced in Powerstown, with a housekeeper to cook and clean, busy with the cattle trade and hunting in the winter, I gave little thought to amending my bachelor status. Little did I realize that others determined that this situation should not continue . . . One such was Cathy Egan of Corduff, compulsive matchmaker. Cathy introduced me to Joan Walsh from Blackrock. Far removed from the cattle business, Joan's family were instead involved in that activity which gave its name to the 1976 Grand National winner—Rag Trade. Actually, Joan's father was a clothes manufacturer with interests in Macys, while Reggie, her brother, was also involved in the clothing trade.

We were duly married in Kilbride in 1957, Reggie

Walsh acting as my best man. Our honeymoon we spent in Scotland, touring the Highlands in an Austin A30. That's when I stopped smoking. It happened when I stopped the Austin outside a shop in the middle of nowhere, prompting Joan to ask why. I said I fancied buying myself a cigarette. When Joan laughingly pointed out that nobody any longer sold single cigarettes in 1957 AD, I took the hint and have never smoked since.

Married life back in Powerstown saw us blessed with five healthy children—Jonathan, Sara, Simon, Rachel and Dominic. Far from following in their family tradition, Jonathan went into marine biology, Sara into the hotel business, Simon into architecture, Rachel into school-teaching and Dominic into marketing. Simon married a fellow architect, Joanna Vergase from Kuala Lumpur, who has given us three adorable granddaughters.

As our children grew up and went their various ways we decided that Powerstown had become too big for our needs. So we sold the house with ten acres, retaining the remainder of the land. Then we spent some idyllic time living in a wing of Carton—one of only four families on the entire estate—surrounded by cattle, a herd of deer and hares as big as lambs. Had it been ours, we would probably be there still. But it wasn't. Development of the Carton estate induced us to move via Straffan to Cormickstown Wood, Maynooth, as pleasant a domicile as anyone could desire.

CHAPTER FIFTEEN

Lucky Houses

U nlike my father, who did not live to realize the astonishing appreciation in value of that 10-acre field he had inadvertently purchased in Foxrock, Johnny Byrne, his friend and rival in the cattle business, did just that.

Rathbeale Hall, Swords, County Dublin, is an early eighteenth-century mansion, built around 1710 by Lieutenant-General Richard Gorges and considerably extended by his son and heir Hamilton Gorges in 1740. His architect is thought to have been Richard Castle, the exceptional quality plasterwork similarly attributed to the Francini brothers. In 1810 Rathbeale was bought by Matthew Corbally, remaining in his family's possession until 1958 when it was sold by the son of the last Corbally to live there, Lady Mary Corbally.

The purchaser was Johnny Byrne; the price paid £17,000. Inevitably, such a pretentious house aroused comment, much of it conveyed to the new owner in somewhat ironic vein. One in particular—Stephen Griffin, well known Suffolk sheep breeder— taunted Johnny that he had been robbed, especially as he now faced a stiff annual bill for domestic rates on a house in which he surely did not propose to reside, in God's name. Whatever about the price he had paid for Rathbeale Hall, Johnny certainly had no intention of making it his residence. The obvious solution was to take the roof off, thereby avoiding any further rates demands.

Johnny summoned his chosen builder and asked him to quote for removing the roof. The man priced the job at £450. Johnny dug in at £350, a price after all being merely an invitation to bid. The builder was adamant. Not for a penny less than £450 would he undertake the task. As Johnny Byrne could not lose face, he had no choice but to abuse and then dismiss the wretch. The roof stayed on. However, time and neglect quickly reduced Rathbeale Hall to semi-dereliction. Johnny Byrne found the elegant hallway convenient for the storage of galvanized iron sheeting, the hall door hanging forlornly ajar.

The Georgian Society, founded coincidentally in 1958 by Desmond Guinness and his wife Mariga to save such as Rathbeale Hall for posterity, went and saw and shook their collective heads and walked away. Rathbeale Hall, they declared, was beyond rescue. That Mariga Guinness should have been a great-grandniece of Elizabeth, Empress of Austria, would hardly, I fear, have unduly troubled Johnny Byrne's conscience over the dilapidation of Rathbeale Hall during his ownership. In any case, Julian Peck and his wife—friends of Chester Beatty— thought otherwise. They bravely gave Johnny Byrne the

£25,000 he demanded and set about the slow, expensive but ultimately triumphant task of restoration.

Just as he had when he purchased the property, Johnny had to endure commiserations on giving the place away for a proverbial song. He had been robbed, for a second time. Johnny was philosophical about his financial 'mishap'. Rounding on Job's comforters—particularly Stephen Griffin—Johnny pointed out, with some acerbity, that he had 'blundered' in paying £17,000 for Rathbeale Hall. To make a bad situation worse, he had erred again in letting it go for a paltry £25,000. However, to Johnny's way of thinking, his two 'blunders' had netted him a cool £8,000, a return of 50% on his original investment. And what the hell was wrong with that?

If further proof were needed that 'money gets money', the purchase of Rathaldron House confirms the truth of that old adage. Wealthy Canadian sportsman Gene Kruger gave £60,000 for this property, a castellated nineteenth-century mansion which incorporates the fifteenth-century square tower that was Rathaldron Castle. Unusually for the Navan vicinity, Rathaldron's acreage was very middling agricultural land. When invited to walk the 200-odd acres and comment to its intending owner, I had to choose my words carefully. To a man of his means the land was incidental. The castle was the thing. 'If you haven't it bought by Friday, I'll be buying it on Monday!'

Luckily for Gene Kruger, it was not the land but what lay beneath it that was to offer potential salvation. Such were the purported deposits of zinc below the surface, Michael Wymes, backed by his father-in-law Tom Roche senior, bid Gene £1m for the property, an offer which the grateful Gene was not slow in accepting. Bemused by these developments, Gene Kruger reflected that he had left his native Canada to escape from mining and now, willy nilly, found that mining had pursued him across the pond. Rather had he settled in Royal Meath to indulge his love of farming and hunting. 'Farming,' Gene declared, 'is the sport of kings!' To which Helena, his wife, riposted: 'Yes. And hunting is the sport of farmers!'

The entrepreneurs formed their mining company on 18th March 1971, naming it after the winner of Cheltenham's Champion Hurdle the previous day—Bula. The subsequent legal battles between Bula Mines and its rival Tara Mines were to make news headlines over the next three decades. Those problems meant that Gene Kruger never did see his money, though he hardly had need of it. Today Rathaldron belongs to his son Joseph.

CHAPTER SIXTEEN

Winners and Losers

As I said earlier, my father was fine with hunting, but racing was quite another matter. He actually thought the Turf far too high profile, attracting publicity which he could certainly do without. Jack Keogh did not subscribe to the maxim that all publicity is good publicity. Still less was he in sympathy with Oscar Wilde's aphorism: 'There is only one thing in the world worse than being talked about, and that is not being talked about.'

So, how did I get the racing bug? Almost certainly from the hunting field, where the majority of the Ward Union regulars were steeped in racing—Tom Dreaper of Kilsallaghan, Ted and Martin Kelly of Greenogue, Dan and Joan Moore in Old Fairyhouse, Standish Collen, Alec Craigie, Silloge House, Finglas, who won the Ward Union Hunt Cup three years in succession (1933-35) on Silloge, and Roy Craigie, Pat Rooney, Bertie Reynolds, all household names for their racecourse successes. Larry King, Crickstown House, bred, reared and hunted Easter Hero, the dual Cheltenham Gold Cup winner. At the opposite end of our country Laurence Geraghty of Pelletstown bred and reared Golden Miller, winner of a record five

Cheltenham Gold Cups and a Grand National. Lord Fingall rode Sir Lindsay to win the 1930 National Hunt Chase at Cheltenham, returning years later as owner of Roddy Owen, successful in the 1959 Gold Cup. Dick Ball of the Naul had bred Reynoldstown, winner of consecutive Grand Nationals. And in the heart of it wasn't the mighty Arkle—'Himself'—bred by the Bakers of Malahow?

Nor was the involvement confined to the 'lean and limber head / hardy, humble bred' of the National Hunt world. Bobby Elwes, Ennistown Stud, Kilmessan, was breeding speedsters like Whistling Wind and Kingsmuir. Bert Kerr, the legendary bloodstock agent, was based in Summerseat, Clonee, where his brother Kevin trained the horses that Bert had yet to sell on. Robert Laidlaw and his daughter Betty, Castleknock, bred and owned big winners under both codes. Norman MacNaughton, Simmonstown Stud, Celbridge, bred and raced countless good winners. Tim Rogers stood some of the best stallions in Ireland at his Airlie Stud, Lucan. John and Eleanor Samuelson had their Cloghran Stud, made famous by the stallion Blandford before the war. Senator John D. Sheridan, farmer and cattle exporter, had his Kilberry Stud near Navan. The Stafford-King-Harmans of Leixlip had horses with John Oxx for decades, as did Brigadier Stewart, Dowdstown Stud, Maynooth. Frankie and Honor Svedjar, equally successful at Ascot or Cheltenham, had their

Clonsilla Stud. John Thursby and his wife had their Irish base at Ballymacarney, The Ward, sending their flat horses to Mickey Rogers and their jumpers to Tom Dreaper. Anne, Duchess of Westminster, had her stud, Bryanstown, Maynooth, where Arkle spent his summers at grass.

Trainers within the Ward Union country included Barney Nugent in The Ward itself, leading trainer in Ireland in the post-war years. Tom Dreaper, Kilsallagan, sent out such as Prince Regent, Arkle and Flyingbolt to give him three of his record ten Irish Grand Nationals, all the while adamant that he was a farmer who trained horses as a sideline. Actually, the Dreaper family had their own stall in the Dublin cattle market, where Tom was to be found on Wednesdays without fail. Jim, his son, would add a further four Irish Nationals to the family's Easter Monday haul at what for many years were entitled the Ward Union Hunt Races. Dan and Joan Moore in Old Fairyhouse tended to target the big Cheltenham meeting, with consistent success. Georgie Wells in Clonee had scored his first ever training success with Umm in the 1955 Irish National. Waring Willis and his wife Iny sent out dozens of winners from their Skryne, Tara, stable. Jimmy Brogan of Rathfeigh never did win the Irish National as a jockey, but gained compensation when saddling Gold Legend to win it in 1958. Clem Magnier, Rathvale, Athboy, upheld that stable's Fairyhouse record created by George Walker and his son Harry by winning the 1953 Irish National with the veteran grey Overshadow. Locally based permit holders—who trained exclusively for their immediate families—included 'Brig' Fowler in Rahinstown, Colonel Newell at Drumree and Jack Prendergast in Kilcock, each of whom won his goodly share of races.

Of course it was highly contagious. Moreover, I now realize that there is no known antidote. Many a man has kicked tobacco, been weaned off alcohol and even drugs. But the racing bug is like malaria. You can get remissions, but never a complete cure. Nevertheless, it was not until 1963 that I felt confident to suggest to my father that the well-bred grey yearling colt by Palestine offered in settlement of a Livestock Credit Corporation account for £1,000 was surely worth taking a chance upon. Nothing doing. Had I really had the courage of my convictions I could have bought that colt when he went for 900 guineas at the Ballsbridge sales that autumn. I had even more opportunity to regret my caution when Green Banner—as he was named—went on to win four times as a two-year-old in Bert Kerr's colours, becoming the third highest rated two-year-old in Ireland in 1964. And it did not stop at that either. Runner up in the Tetrarch Stakes at the Curragh on his seasonal début in 1965, Green Banner returned to the Curragh to run clean away with the Irish 2,000 Guineas, worth £7,706 to the winning owners, Bert Kerr and Mrs

Carole McGrane, Santa Fe, California. It doubtless cost Mrs McGrane an awful lot more than her share of the prize money to buy out Bert and ship Green Banner to California to continue his racing career out there.

Not until 1973 did I register my distinctive 'White, beige stag's head, red cap' colours—a design one simply would not be permitted today—to begin my career as an owner with Curragh trainer Stuart Murless. Stuart was rarely parted from his pipe, referred to by his friends as the 'Slough gasworks'. Training since 1946, Stuart had developed a preference for American-breds, claiming that they were more precocious and thus more likely to win as two-year-olds than their European counterparts. Pepi Image fitted that bill, costing us $26,500 at the Florida-Breds Two-year-olds in Training Sales. Second to one of Vincent O'Brien's at the Phoenix Park at the beginning of July, Pepi Image made handsome amends when winning over the course and distance three weeks later. A model of consistency, she ran Noble Mark to a neck in the Phoenix '1500'—the Irish juvenile sprint championship—caught a proper Tartar when second to Gentle Thoughts at the Curragh and finished her first season when second again to Milly Whiteway in the inaugural running of the Moyglare Stakes. Timeform described Pepi Image as 'very useful', giving her a rating of 111.

That same autumn I made my first foray to the Kentucky sales, in search of foals to resubmit as yearlings either in

Dublin or Newmarket. The term 'pinhooker' had not yet entered the horsey vocabulary. In hindsight—famously twenty-twenty vision—that move may have been prompted by the closure of the Dublin cattle market. That landmark event in the Keogh family's history took place on Wednesday, 9 May 1973, 110 years after it had opened. A measure of the changes that had taken place in the cattle business can be gauged from a survey carried out for 1917. It showed that in that particular year the Dublin cattle market had handled 200,000 cattle and 300,000 sheep. On Wednesday, 9 May 1973, just 325 animals were sold there. The rapid growth of cattle marts throughout the country had siphoned off the traditional sources of supply.

Vincent O'Brien, Tom Cooper, Robert Sangster, John Magnier and their associates had pioneered the American market in their quest to repatriate the best British and Irish bloodlines, intent on sourcing baby racehorses to make into stallions on the strength of their racecourse achievements. However, cattlemen such as John Hayden and I were more concerned with buying foals to turn a quicker profit.

While in Bluegrass country we came across Ted Curtin, then training in Ireland for Nelson Bunker Hunt, the colourful, opinionated Texan millionaire, who set out to corner the world silver market. Bunker obviously found horse dealing hungry business, calling for vast platters of food, cleared with gusto. A typical Hayden quip prompted by this spectacle brought a memorable rejoinder from Ted Curtin. 'Eat, is it? That man would eat the picture of the Last Supper!'

Beginner's luck? No matter, the prospect of the Irish 1,000 Guineas fairly shortened that winter. She would have won it too, had the English stayed away! As it was, Pepi Image ran the race of her career to finish third to the raiders Gaily and Northern Gem. Still, to be placed in a classic with your very first runner of any description is pretty special. Naturally, we kept Pepi Image as the foundation mare for our newly-formed stud at Powerstown. President Elect, her first foal, won three times in Joan's colours. National Image gave Joan two more wins, while National Form more than played his part, winning both the 1985 Irish Cambridgeshire and the valuable Hennessy Handicap at Leopardstown. Trained by Noel Meade, National Form carried the colours of Turform Limited. That was the Irish equivalent of Timeform, an enterprise in which I had taken a substantial share, believing that Irish racegoers warranted such a service and were prepared to pay for it.

I'm getting ahead of myself in recounting Pepi Image's offspring and their achievements. Her initial racecourse achievements had tempted Denis Coakley—joint master with me in the Ward Union—to try his luck. Denis really did experience beginner's luck, for his Fleeting Hind made a winning début at the Phoenix Park in Horse Show Week 1974. By then we had been joined by Denis and Anne O'Kelly, both of whom visited the winner's enclosure in 1975 through the exploits of Leinster Leader, King's Path and Raw Recruit, all of them USA-bred and all of them trained by Stuart Murless in Loughbrown Lodge, right beside the Curragh racecourse. That same year I had a 'leg' (quarter share) in National Wish. Carrying the colours of Dr J. Masterson and trained by Stuart, National Wish—yet another USA-bred—won a Group 3 at the Curragh. Better still, he went on to justify favouritism in the Group 2 Phoenix '1500', the race in which Pepi Image had finished second for me two seasons previously.

Keeping the best wine till last, am I? Well, yes, I suppose I am. Denis Coakley and I had become really and truly hooked on this racing game. We wanted to win classic races, so we did. To this end we persuaded Denis O'Kelly to divert the money he had earmarked for buying a farm into the purchase of yearlings bred to win at the top level. Think of the return on investment! Between the three of us we bought a grey filly by Supreme Sovereign for 6,200 guineas and a chestnut colt by Sea Bird II for 22,000 guineas. It was agreed that the filly would carry Anne O'Kelly's colours, while the colt would race in Denis Coakley's livery. The colt we named Sea Break and the filly Nocturnal Spree.

Stuart Murless could be said to have proved his point about the relative backwardness of our European-breds, as this pair did not see a racecourse until September 1974. And when they did it was against each other, in a Curragh event for unraced animals. Neither was particularly fancied. Nonetheless, Sea Break ran out the ready winner, with Nocturnal Spree finishing third. Who could ask for more?

As it happened, Nocturnal Spree split a pastern, which put an end to her juvenile campaign. On the credit side, Sea Break went on to run a blinder when second to the French colt Green Desert in the Observer Gold Cup at Doncaster, enough to see him top-rated in the Irish Free Handicap. We may have lost the run of ourselves, for we turned down an offer of $250,000 for a half-share in Sea Break that winter. When I think of it now, the Dáil had been plunged into uproar when the Government of the day had authorized the Irish National Stud to give the Aga Khan £250,000 for his Derby and St Leger winner Tulyar only twenty years previously.

Things all happened rather more quickly in 1975. Stuart had the pair ready in jig time. Nocturnal Spree reappeared to win a Curragh maiden on 5 April. One week later Sea Break won the Group 3 Vauxhall Trial Stakes at the Phoenix Park as an odds-on shot should. Bring on the Guineas at Newmarket! The 1,000 Guineas opened proceedings on Thursday, 1 May, 16 runners. Rose Bowl, Lester Piggott's mount, was 7/4 favourite, while Nocturnal Spree, with Johnnie Roe on board, was easy to back at 14/1. To cut to the chase, as they say, Rose Bowl got no run of the race whatever, the door slammed in Lester's face everywhere he tried to get through, whereas Nocturnal Spree ran her heart out to pip the French filly Girl Friend by the shortest of short heads. I thought the judge would never call that photo finish, half dreading the outcome, for nobody was prepared to preempt him. He called it right.

Could our outrageous good fortune hold good for forty-eight hours? It did not, Sea Break finishing only twelfth to Bolkonski, Henry Cecil's first classic winner. Grundy finished second, *en route* to winning the Derby, the Irish Derby and the King George VI and Queen Elizabeth Stakes. Sadly, neither Nocturnal Spree nor Sea Break managed to win again. Sea Break, being a son of the outstanding French champion Sea Bird II, went to France as stallion. However, Nocturnal Spree almost quadrupled her Guineas stake when fetching 96,000 guineas at the Newmarket sales, becoming in the process the third most expensive filly sold in England to that point. As all good poker players should, we left the gaming tables, counting our money.

Whereas those flat yearlings had been purposefully bought, my next racehorse became mine on a whim.

Yasmin Allen of Ballymaloe House Hotel, whom I had come to know during our annual summer vacations down there, became one of the first female apprentices to ride winners in Ireland. She had only moved on to France when Richard Annesley, her boss on the Curragh, decided to give up training before it cost him any more money.

In the course of working for trainer Mick Bartholemew 'Yaz' fell in love with a little chestnut gelding named Irian. As she subsequently told the Irish racing press: 'In France Irian was a nervous wreck. Mind you, you cannot blame him. French racing would drive anyone mad. One day he broke a blood vessel in a race and I offered the owner £280. He accepted there and then, no bargaining, nothing.'

Yasmin managed to hitch a lift for herself and her horse on the plane carrying the French runner, El Badr, over for the 1978 Irish Derby. On landing at Dublin airport, Yasmin contacted me, knowing I lived nearby. I was so intrigued by her tale that I offered to take Irian off her hands for whatever amount he now stood her. So, for £900 Irian became mine and Yasmin caught the next plane back to Paris.

I gave my whimsical purchase the summer off and sent him to Arthur Moore. His first run, in Tralee, was simply dreadful. Fortunately, his next few runs showed great improvement, so much so that he started favourite when successful at Leopardstown over Christmas and at Punchestown in January, ridden each time by Arthur's claiming amateur, Mr 'Bay' Cockburn. The partnership clicked again at Killarney in July 1979, before Tommy Carberry took over to win a valuable sponsored hurdle on him at Tralee. When the weights came out for the Irish Sweeps Hurdle at Leopardstown at Christmas Arthur seemed to think Irian might just have a pound or two in hand of the handicapper. But there could be no question of the rider putting up overweight.

Tommy Carberry could have done the weight (10 st.) with no trouble at all, but he was committed to ride Straight Row for Jim Dreaper. Maybe give Bay the chance? Why not, provided he could make the weight. Poor Bay starved himself right throughout Christmas, only to admit on the eve of the race that the scales had beaten him. Arthur turned to another amateur, Ann Ferris. Starting at 25/1, Ann and Irian held on to beat 'Blackie' Quinn on the favourite, Twinburn, winning the most valuable hurdle race in Ireland by a short head. The Sweeps Hurdle was worth £19,714 to the winner, a fair return on the £900 he had cost me to take him off Yasmin's hands.

The handicapper duly took his revenge, for Irian failed even to make the frame throughout 1980. If he had any future, it was over fences, despite his lack of size. However, in racehorses it is the engine that counts and Irian duly scored over fences at Navan in February 1981, even if he did give Tommy Carberry several scary moments in the process. Arthur suggested a crack at Aintree, but over the park course fences. Frank Berry had the mount and Irian ran well to finish second to Cecil Ronaldson's runner Foxbat. Sadly for Cecil, Foxbat was adjudged to have hampered our horse on the run from the last. We were awarded the Skol Chase in the stewards' room, never a nice way to win a race. But thus it was.

Since Irian's time I have been granted a few remissions from what Edward O'Grady calls: 'the game that tames lions'. However, those remissions would seem to be over just now. Following my fortunate escape from what I call my 'twenty-four-hour cancer' in 2003 I was advised to take a sunshine holiday. As Joan had relations in Sydney, that seemed an obvious destination. Of course I had to experience Australian racing. . . An introduction to jumping trainer John O'Connor, whose family had emigrated from Tipperary, who assured me that well-bred cast-offs from the flat scene could be bought for a song, set me thinking about investing in geldings by shuttling stallions, familiar to Irish and English trainers, and bringing them up here for resale. Then the Irish economic bubble burst. End of that notion, as I thought.

John O'Connor wasn't going to let me off the hook. He offered to train my horses for nothing, sharing their winnings fifty-fifty. And that's how I became the leading jumping owner in southern Australia, with just eight horses in training. Admittedly, Murray Bridge, near Adelaide, is a far cry from Cheltenham or Punchestown, but it's good fun. And it's free, at least to me.

It is pretty well impossible to go racing in Australia without hearing stories about the legendary Kerry Packer, mostly to do with his gambling exploits. This one I particularly enjoy. Kerry rolled into Vegas to play the tables. His reputation preceded him and he lacked nothing for solicitous helpmates, plying him with champagne, cigars and flattery. A loudmouthed Texan took umbrage, squaring up to the foreigner. 'Hey, mister. I'm worth $100 million. What you got to say?' Kerry barely looked up. 'That so? How's about I toss you for it.' Exit badly chastened Texan.

John O'Connor has a wry way of putting things. On one occasion he telephoned to say that he was taking one of our horses to run at a major meeting, two days' drive away. Still unaccustomed to the marathon journeys Australia involves, I enquired whether he took his wife with him on those odysseys. 'Sure do. Less trouble than kissin' her goodbye!'

CHAPTER SEVENTEEN

Code Breaker Hayes

Various years stick in individuals' minds for all sorts of reasons. In my own case one such will ever be 1976. The year that my father passed away, aged 74, was also the finest summer that I can recall. After a harsh and bitter spring the wind died away, the sun came out and so remained until the end of October. To my amusement, people became distinctly ratty from the utterly unaccustomed absence of rain. Would that damned sun never stop shining, never give us all a break from the relentless cheerfulness of it all. Unwise to point out that the same moaners might never experience such a summer again.

Coincidentally, Richard Hayes, my uncle through marriage to my Aunt Claire, also died that year, likewise aged 74. Of course we knew of his remarkable academic career, which led on to widespread recognition as Director of the National Library, for which he was awarded honorary doctorates from both Trinity College and the National University of Ireland. To all intents, Richard Hayes' life had been an open book, just as my father's had been. Well, so we believed, until the obituaries began to appear.

Take this excerpt from *The Irish Times*, initialled 'A. Mc.L.'. 'During the war years he enjoyed a phantom rank in the Army and was active in counter-intelligence. His linguistic skills (his earliest published work was on the little-known comparative idiom, 1927) and innate gifts of mental organisation and memory made him an outstanding success as a cipher-breaker and he was a leading figure in the interception of messages which led to the collapse of all the German attempts to establish an intelligence network in Ireland. Among other successes, he organised the 'double-cross' (by a flow of fictitious messages) of Dr Herman Goertz,the leading Abwehr agent. It can now be told that the initials 'H.G.' subscribed to a review in this paper of Stephan's 'Spies in Ireland' were a pseudonym for Dr Hayes adopted as a tribute to the memory of Goertz, with whom he had become quite friendly.

'Although so busy in undercover operations, Dr Hayes by no means neglected his official duties, and it was in this period that the National Library acquired such outstanding items as the Ormonde papers from Kilkenny Castle, the tens of thousands of old photographic plates of the Lawrence collection, the records of the old Office of the Ulster King-of-Arms which, as the Genealogical Office, became part of the National Library in 1943, and the manuscripts of the early novels of George Bernard Shaw. These last were elicited by a characteristically brief and witty letter from Hayes: 'Dear Bernard Shaw, I can think of no better place than the National Library of

Ireland for your manuscripts and first editions. Can you?'

Even though the Second World War had ended thirty years before Uncle Richard passed away, sensitivity related to intelligence and counter-intelligence remained so acute that the veil of silence, lifted so briefly to acknowledge Richard Hayes' role in code-breaking, dropped again as quickly. Files remained classified. Silence reigned. On the rare occasion that the subject surfaced at all, it tended to be posed as a query: 'Who were we neutral against?' That was until 2003, when *MI5 and Ireland 1939-1945—The Official History* was published. It revealed the links between MI5 and Irish Military Intelligence (G2), specifically with 'Liam Archer, Dan Bryan and Joe Guilfoyle, and G2's code expert Dr Richard Hayes.' What went unnoticed by MI5—or so at least it appeared—was that the key Irish figures involved 'Liam Archer, Dan Bryan and Richard Hayes all had extensive War of Independence experience as clandestine operators.'

The publication of that report, initiated by MI5, resurrected the tricky issue of Eire's purported neutrality during what was termed here the 'Emergency'. The *Sunday Tribune* assigned Fiona Looney to investigate. 'As far as MI5 was concerned, "his gifts amount to genius". The BBC producer researching his life calls him "a Colossus of a man—Ireland's greatest unsung hero". Gunther Schutz, one of the most notorious German spies interned in Ireland during the war, described him as "absolutely brilliant".

'As far as Schutz and the other German spies whose cells he entered during the Emergency knew, their quiet-spoken and polite interrogator was "Captain Grey", a mysterious military figure always accompanied by another intelligence officer. Only a handful of of people in G2, army intelligence, knew that Grey, one of the most important and prolific code-breakers of the Second World War, was not a military man at all. His real name was Richard Hayes, and he was director of the National Library.

'It is only in recent years that the importance and extent of Hayes's work has become known. During the Emergency, even his own family didn't know the exact nature of his role with military intelligence. His daughter Faery [Claire], aged seven when the war broke out, only learned recently that her father used her school exercise book to decode complex German ciphers. Even Gunther Schutz went to his grave in 1991 still believing it was another man, Commandant de Butleir, who was responsible for identifying his microdot codes—the first cryptologist in the world to do so.

'But it was Hayes who spotted Schutz's codes. In all 30 pages of operating instructions as well as extensive lists of Nazi sympathisers in the Republic were secreted in random characters in newspaper cuttings that the German intelligence agent was carrying when he was picked up by gardai in Wexford in 1941.

'Schutz—dropped into Ireland to make contact with IRA

members sympathetic to the German cause and to transmit weather reports back to his handlers in Hamburg—readily gave up one of his codes to his Irish captors in the hope of diverting attention from his microdots, but a microscope in his luggage raised the suspicions of the authorities and his belongings were handed over to Hayes.

'He studied two newspaper cuttings tucked into the spy's pocket book and in a testimonial letter affirming the curative qualities of Aspro, he identified messages, reduced in size 400 times, and secreted within three letter 'o's in the text. On an article about Oxford Pamphlets he spotted a further four microdots, with three more in an ad for the Green Park Hotel. Within 10 days of Schutz's arrest, Hayes had found and translated the entire contents of his highly-sensitive microdots. It would take the FBI a further four months to even identify that such a system of transmitting messages existed.

'"The Germans were so cocksure that the microdots couldn't be discovered that they didn't even encode them," Schutz said after the war. "They were to be a vital weapon in espionage. Finding them as the Irish intelligence officers did was an act of brilliance."

'Hayes had some success decoding cable messages, but it was working on complex letter-based ciphers that he demonstrated his brilliance as a code-breaker. When Major Hermann Goertz, the most senior Nazi agent to be captured in Ireland, was arrested at the end of 1941, he was carrying a code later described by MI5 as "one of the best three or four in the war". A similar cipher had already baffled cryptologists at Bletchley Park, the headquarters of British code-breaking activity, but Hayes finally identified a system of decoding it based on a sequence of rotating keywords. The first of the Goertz messages to be successfully decoded was unlocked with the key "Cathleen Ni Houlihan".

'Informed of the breakthrough Hayes had made, Cecil Liddell of MI5 visited Dublin in 1943 and the two secret services continued to share intelligence information until the end of the war. Afterwards Liddell said that there was a "whole series of ciphers that couldn't have been solved without Hayes's input".'

Aunt Claire had predeceased Uncle Richard in 1969, survived by their sons Mervyn and Jimmy, daughters Joan and Claire, known as 'Faery'. They had married in 1928. What if anything my aunt ever knew of her husband's earlier activities she took with her. My father would have been horrified to think of his sister bringing anyone of 'extensive War of Independence as clandestine operators' into the firmly apolitical Keogh family. As for his later involvement in military intelligence and code-breaking, that came as a shock to everybody. However, if it did, these revelations conferred a lasting glow of reflected glory upon Uncle Richard's extended family.

CHAPTER EIGHTEEN

Put it there!

'All the world's a stage,
And all the men and women merely players:
They have their exits and their entrances;
And one man in his time plays many parts,
His acts being seven ages.'

AS YOU LIKE IT

How that fragment of Shakespeare got into my head and there remained I simply cannot recall. Perhaps those Jesuits in Clongowes Wood long ago deserve the credit, or the blame. Nevertheless, The Bard was on the money. Mind you, having re-read the rest of that soliloquy, I think it best to leave it at that! Who would hasten the onset of 'Sans teeth, sans eyes, sans taste, sans everything'?

'And one man in his time plays many parts.' True that is, as I hope this account of my life and times has managed to convey. Wheeling and dealing, hunting and racing, family and finance comprise those many parts. Some survive, essentially unchanged throughout my four-score years. Others – particularly the very nature of the core cattle trade – have changed beyond recognition. Even writing about the Dublin Cattle Market and those country fairs, with the vital parts they played in our national economy, makes me feel like some sort of dinosaur.

But then, time never does stand still. And precisely because time does not stand still I felt an obligation to put my experiences between covers to leave a record of how things were, so that those who come after me may discover, as and if they choose to look.

Long gone the days of haggling over cattle with wily farmers, the inevitable tangler 'making the deal', until at length you thrust out your hand, spat on it to seal the deal and cried out manfully: 'Put it there!'

Acknowledgements

In putting my memoirs together I have begged and borrowed from many and varied sources too numerous to thank by name. Their authors deserve my thanks for making *Cattleman* the book it has thus become. Similarly with the photographs and other images that struck me as deserving inclusion in these pages. Their provenance is so varied that it has proved simply impossible to identify their sources in all but a few instances. I should like to think that those who do recognize their unattributed handiwork will accept this as my sincere act of acknowledgement.

Bibliography

AALEN, WHELAN & STOUT, Eds. – *Atlas of the Irish Rural Landscape*, CUI, Cork, 1997

BARDON, Jonathan – *History of Ireland in 250 Episodes*, Gill & Macmillan, Dublin 2008

BELL, J. & WATSON, M. – *A History of Irish Farming*, Four Courts, Dublin, 2008

BENCE-JONES, Mark – *Twilight of the Ascendancy*, Constable, London, 1987

BUCKLEY, Ciaran, WARD, Chris – *Strong Farmer*, Liberties Press, Dublin 2007

CARROLL, Joseph – *Ireland 1939-1945*, David & Charles, Newton Abbot, 1975

COLGAN, John – *Leixlip, County Kildare*, Tyrconnell Press, Leixlip, 2005

CONNOLLY, S.J., Editor – *Oxford Companion to Irish History*, Oxford University Press, 2002

CRAIG, Patricia, Editor – *The Oxford Book of Ireland*, Oxford University Press, 1998

CRAIGIE, Eric – *An Irish Sporting Life*, Lilliput Press, Dublin, 1994

CRONIN, Maurice – *Deasy, Rickard* – Dictionary of Irish Biography, RIA, 2009

DOOLEY, Terence – *The Decline of the Big House in Ireland*, Wolfhound, Dublin, 2001

DWYER, T. Ryle – *Big Fellow, Long Fellow*, Gill & Macmillan, Dublin, 1999

FEEHAN, John – *Farming in Ireland*, UCD Faculty of Agriculture, Dublin, 2003

FITZPATRICK, Bernard – *Irish Sport and Sportsmen*, M.H. Gill & Son, Dublin, 1878

GUINNESS, Desmond & RYAN, Wm – *Irish Houses & Castles*, Thames & Hudson, London, 1971

HOYSTED, Frank – *Reminiscences of a Chauffeur*, Privately printed, 1992

JOYCE, Weston St John – *The Neighbourhood of Dublin*, M.H. Gill & Son, Dublin, 1912

KELLY, Fergus – *Early Irish Farming,* School of Celtic Studies, Dublin, 1997

LACEY, Jim – *History of the Barony of Castleknock*, Mercier Press, Cork, 2007

LUCAS, A.T. – *Cattle in Ancient Ireland*, Boethius Press, Kilkenny, 1989

LYNCH, Stanislaus – *Echoes of the Hunting Horn*, Talbot Press, Dublin, 1946

LYONS, J.B. – *Brief Lives of Irish Doctors*, Blackwater Press, Dublin, 1978

MacDONNELL, Randal – *The Lost Houses of Ireland*, Weidenfeld & Nicolson, London, 2002

McKAY, Sinclair – *The Secret Life of Bletchley Park*, Aurum Press, London, 2010

McMANUS, Ruth – *Dublin 1910-1940, The City & Suburbs*, Four Courts Press, Dublin, 2002

McREDMOND, Louis, Editor – *Modern Irish Lives*, Gill & Macmillan, Dublin, 1996

MANNING, Maurice – *James Dillon – A Biography*, Wolfhound, Dublin, 2000

MAXWELL, Constantia – *Dublin under the Georges*, George G. Harrap, London, 1936

MURPHY, David – *Deasy, Maj H.H.* – Dictionary of Irish Biography, RIA, 2009

O'CONNOR, Ulick – *Oliver St John Gogarty*, Obolensky, New York, 1963

O'CONNOR MORRIS, M – *Hibernia Hippica*, Harrison & Sons, London, 1900

O'HALPIN, Eunan – *MI5 and Ireland 1939-1945*, Irish Academic Press, Dublin, 2003

O'KELLY, Gerard A. – *The Dublin Cattle Market, 1863-1973*, Unicorn Films, Dublin, 1973

O'TOOLE, Jimmy – *The Carlow Gentry*, Privately printed, Carlow, 1993

QUISH, John A. – *Going to the Creamery*, Creamery Press, Bishopstown, Cork, 2010

REGAN, Michael A. – *Ten in a Bed*, Abbeyview Press, Trim, County Meath, 2006

ROSS, David – *Ireland – History of a Nation*, Geddes & Grosset, New Lanark, 2005

SOMERVILLE-LARGE, Peter – *The Irish Country House*, Sinclair-Stevenson, London, 1995

SOMERVILLE-LARGE, Peter – *Dublin – The Fair City*, Sinclair-Stevenson, London, 1996

WELCOME, John – *The Sporting Empress*, Michael Joseph, London, 1975

WILLS, Clair – *That Neutral Island*, Faber & Faber, London, 2007